Mystery of Emptiness & Love provides a fresh and insightful commentary on the nature of reality. Timeless Buddhist teachings combined with an original perspective illuminate the illusory nature of how we are alive, and provide a careful analysis for one to arrive at the correct view of emptiness. Her commentary on Chandrakirti's Twenty Emptinesses is offered with easy-to-read and concise explanations. This is a gem of a book for anyone contemplating the nature of reality.

Betty J. Kramer, PhD University of Wisconsin-Madison
Author of *Living through loss: Interventions across the life span*

Domo Geshe Rinpoche has finally put into the written word a dharmic path comprehensible to our western minds. With these words she also guides us towards a heart-understanding for which no words exist; a healing so profound that no medicine can touch it!

Capri Fillmore, MD, MPH, MSc, Acoma, NM

The gap between obscure ancient scholarly languages and modern western views has been difficult to close. Into this gap comes *Mystery of Emptiness & Love* by Domo Geshe Rinpoche. Rinpoche explains the Twenty Emptinesses of Chandrakirti, breathtakingly interwoven with the development of altruistic great compassion. This work will someday be considered seminal in transmission of dharma to the west.

Mitzi A. Forbes, PhD

Other books by Domo Geshe Rinpoche
Red Lotus Buddhist Wisdom
ISBN 978-0-692-00410-4

Hermitage Buddhist Publishing
PO Box 126
Neillsville, WI 54456

Library of Congress registered copyright 2009
Tara Wangchuk,
Domo Geshe Rinpoche
www.white-conch.org hermitagebuddhistpublishing@gmail.com
First edition
Printed in the United States of America
ISBN: 978-0-692-00394-7

Mystery
of
Emptiness & Love

By Domo Geshe Rinpoche

Dedicated to my teachers

Great Sera Je Geshe Jampa Chombe
(1909-1959)
and
Kyabie Trijang Rinpoche
(1900-1981)

and to the long life of **His Holiness the Dalai Lama**

I wish to thank Sarah Buchler (Ani Ngawang Gema) for her work in final editing, as well as others too many to name here for kindly reading and correcting any grammar errors in the text. However, I take full responsibility for content. Every attempt was made to credit sources for quotations.

Table of Contents

Introduction   1

Part one: The Dumbing Down of Our Original Nature 3

Chapter 1 Doubt is Good!   4

How will I be after enlightenment?   5
Search for truth   6
Lorig: Buddhist mind training   7
Skillful doubt is easier than deluded doubt   9

Chapter 2 Demystifying Emptiness   12

Subtle is stronger   14
Buddhist scholarly explanation of the innate view   15
Refutation of Buddhist scholarship by Western students   16
Two methods: Inner outer based views of inquiry   18
The runaway horse of the untamed mind   19
A simpler method   20
Buddhist logical discernment   21

Chapter 3 The Real You   24

You are not the one you think you are   25
Emanation is a natural process   26
The purpose of life   27
Energetic closure for fresh beginning   28
Receiving healing and bestowals   29
The cost of human life   30

Chapter 4 The Hypnosis of the Innate View   32

Our worldview   33
Five aspects of the innate view   34
    A perceived separation   35
    Confidence of solidity   35
    Hypnotic blinders   36
    Simplified parameters   36
    Projecting perceptions on others   37
How the innate view damages evolutionary development   38
Forgetting or losing the instructions   39
Nice dharma becoming dry or solidified   40

Chapter 5 Buddhism & the Ego   42

The end of self-cherishing   43

The need for a mentor 44
How the innate view helps evolutionary development 44
We learn compassion by stages 45

Part two: Commentary on Chandrakirti's Twenty Emptinesses Analysis of Non-inherent Existence 47

Chapter 6 Faith in Logic 48

Cultivated faith and trust 49
Destruction of error 50
Agenda 51
Emptiness and Nagarjuna 52
Nagarjuna and Chandrakirti The holy father and son 53
Nagarjuna's important contributions 54
Your aunties' old needlepoint 55

Chapter 7 Learning Reality 58

Point 1: Emptiness of the inner: 60
The correct view 61
Inner bases 62
Reality and falling asleep in meditation 63
Point 2: Emptiness of the outer: 65
Reality, self- cherishing, and misplaced hope 67

Chapter 8 Reality & the Dreamlike World 70

Form's nature is emptiness 72
Reality and that nameless thing 73
Point 3: Emptiness of the inner and the outer: 74
Point 4: Emptiness of emptiness: 75
Point 5: Emptiness of the great: 76
The cosmos 77
Point 6: Emptiness of the ultimate: 78
Reality and heaven 79

Chapter 9 Reality & the Grid of Manifestation 82

Point 7: Emptiness of the composite: 82
Death and rebirth 84
Repairing karmic damage 85
Interior grids of manifestation 86
Reality and the cosmos 86
Ordinary siddhas of magic 88
Previous training 89

Chapter 10 Reality &God — 92

Point 8: Emptiness of the uncomposite: — 92
Long lived gods — 95
God will not be angry — 95
Point 9: Emptiness of that which is beyond extremes: — 97
Two views: existence or non-existence — 98
Point 10: Emptiness of neither beginning nor end: — 100
Dignity in the rain — 101

Chapter 11 Reality &Your Religious Bell — 104

Point 11: Emptiness of what should not be discarded: — 104
Bodhichitta and the mentor — 105
Point 12: Emptiness of the true nature: — 107
Reality and early science systems — 109
Point 13: Emptiness of all phenomena: — 110
A way to describe a cup — 112

Chapter 12 Reality &Keeping Ducks in a Row — 116

Point 14: Emptiness of defining characteristics: — 117
Nirvana and space — 117
Do not damage phenomena — 118
Point 15: Emptiness of the imperceptible: — 118
The flow of pleasant NOW — 119
Time — 120
Holding away change — 120
Point 16: Emptiness that is the absence of entities: — 121
Self does not arise without a function — 122
Self does not exist without a function — 122
We cannot prevent naming — 122
A new kind of self — 123

Chapter 13 Summary of Sixteen Emptinesses — 126

Point one: Emptiness of entities — 127
Point two: Emptiness of nonentities — 128
Point three: Emptiness of the nature — 129
Point four: Emptiness of the entity that is other — 130

Part three: Unfolding the Mystery of Emptiness and Love — 131

Chapter 14 Compassion of Wisdom Bodhisattva — 132

Protected by the innate view — 134

Dharmakaya 135
Great compassion 136
Bodhisattvas learn how to use the senses 137
The Bodhisattva finally enters perfection 138
What is a sentient being? 140

Chapter 15 Compassion of Wisdom

toward the Shaky Mind 142

Rare and special alignment 143
Respecting the mentor and yourself 144
Self-cherishing and trust 145
Making the Bodhisattva into a devil 146
This is not Baby Buddhism 147
Personality and ego 147
Higher insight and love 148
Loving hobbies such as Buddhism 149
Love in the personal liberation vehicle 150
Love in the Mahayana altruistic vehicle 151
Love of study and practice 153
Our thankas and prayer beads 154
The dog's tooth 156
Vast wishes for all sentient beings 157

Chapter 16 Emptiness and Protecting Our Love 160

Integrate knowledge- relax body & mind 161
The membrane separates ordinary mind 162
Strengthen by personal responsibility 164
Power of love 165

Chapter 17 Emptiness &Altruistic Love 168

Loving kindness and the state without foundation 169
Natural altruism 170
Overcoming obstacles to altruistic love 171
Holding all sentient beings in the heart 172
Repairing contaminated energies 173
Sentient beings are near and dear to us 173

Chapter 18 Emptiness & Bliss; Mystery Solved 176

Healing by bliss 177
Bonding Bliss and Emptiness 179
Dynamic redux of bliss-love 179

Introduction

There are Buddhist centers in nearly every town and city, yet most people who are interested in spiritual development never walk into one. You may be like them, researching on your own for many years before deciding to enter a group setting. Perhaps you will never meet Buddhists face to face, choosing instead to read and contemplate deep questions at your own pace. Whether studying on your own or under the guidance of a mentor, this book will assist you in uncovering answers to some of the deepest questions posed by philosophers and sincere thinkers about the nature of reality (i.e., what is real). Based on common sense, using straightforward language and with correct Buddhist reasoning, this guide will encourage you to put into practice the analysis of reality, rather than simply acquiring more knowledge. This book will also act as a guide to many important points regarding the core of Buddhist philosophy, compassion combined with the nature of reality, or "emptiness."

Part One defines the problem sentient beings face with understanding the nature of reality. This predicament results because the innate view causes us to see ourselves and the world around us in a way that is not consistent with the way it actually exists. Because of the innate view, we experience suffering that moves from imperceptible to manifest, while remaining in a kind of sleep-like inner stupor or hypnosis. Waking up from that hypnosis is called "enlightenment," and the name "Buddha" means "The Awakened One." Our confusion regarding reality requires us to move through many steps to understand the illusory nature of how we are alive. In Part One, a frank description of how we are alive is presented from an uncomplicated inner-based view. The programming keeping ordinary beings in the unenlightened state is called the innate view. Because it is important to understand the function of the innate view along with its dysfunction to achieve a balanced view, both limitations and benefits of this special programming are explored in Part One.

Part Two contains the step-by-step method by which the innate view is dismantled. We arrive at the correct view through careful, sequential elimination of incorrect views. The arguments are presented in the form of short excerpts and my commentary based on "Twenty Emptinesses" by Chandrakirti, (600–c. 650), a small but important segment of Chandrakirti's seminal Introduction to the Middle Way, Madhyamakavatara.

Part two is based upon a series of teachings I gave in the summer of 2007 at the White Conch retreat setting, the Hermitage in Wisconsin. This book also grew from Buddhist teachings given over the years in various White Conch Dharma Centers, and continued reflection during its preparation for publication. It reflects my view. I have made great effort to use comprehensible terminology so that formal Buddhist education is not required to follow the logic or perform the analysis. It does not matter what religion you ascribe to or whether you identify with any religion at all. Reality is beyond the confines of all descriptions, methods of discovery and philosophies.

Part Three places the analysis of emptiness in harmony with the teachings of compassion and spiritual love. We learn how the bodhisattva heroes, enlightened beings on their way to perfect Buddhahood, think and behave. Their understanding of the illusory nature of reality might logically make them stern and unforgiving, but they are quite the opposite. How do they train themselves in love?

Part One

The Dumbing Down of our Original Nature

Chapter 1
Doubt is Good!
(Discovering what I really think)

"Monks, we who look at the whole and not just the part, know that we too are systems of interdependence, of feelings, perceptions, thoughts, and consciousness all interconnected. Investigating in this way, we come to realize that there is no me or mine in any one part, just as a sound does not belong to any one part of the lute."
Samyutta Nikaya, from *Buddha Speaks*

We begin a facilitated journey of inquiry into the nature of reality by thinking gently concerning our personal attitudes on this state others call enlightenment. We will need to access our own beliefs in order to uncover attitudes that may be preventing us from higher development.

This important step in changing to become the one you always thought you could be, is an evolutionary development pushing you from somewhere deep inside to make that change. All living beings are undergoing this process right now, but the later stages of change before the event of transformation will require more personal effort. It is often said that when the student is ready, the teacher will appear. In a way that is true, but inside there are changes, new feelings of dissatisfaction, and confusion regarding direction that face the person beginning spiritual search.

In deep, silent meditation retreat, after a great deal of effort, a meditator can sometimes reach a level where he or she perceives or reveals their own personally held view of reality. However, rather than being a comfort and delight, this unveiling can come as a very big surprise to them. According to experiences of many who have entered the enlightened state, it is said that we need to discover what we actually believe in the hidden mind, no matter how politically incorrect or embarrassingly juvenile that might be. Only then are we able to change it toward a healthier model. This revealing or exposing the view is preliminary inner work and is associated with the innate view of believing what is not real to be real.

The purpose of this book is to help you uncover the view that is holding you, rather than the view that you are holding. Anyone can do the process of analysis described, as well as the meditations needed to stabilize more healthy perceptions, during which time many layers of fantasy will be exposed and discarded. An important fantasy that many meditators hold is the dream that enlightenment will be an answer to end all difficulties and that they will be happy forever. However, enlightenment is not perfection; it only gets you to the platform where you can begin to work in earnest.

How will I be after enlightenment?

Because enlightenment is something that you have not yet experienced, there are many unusual ideas you can develop toward that state. There are people who are actually afraid of enlightenment because they believe that they will disappear like a puff of smoke once they become enlightened. Therefore, although they try to meditate, they are not very good at it because inside themselves, they are afraid they might actually gain enlightenment and disappear, which they are not ready to do. I have also heard more than once, *"If I become enlightened, I won't care any more about my wife, my husband or my children. And since I do care about them, I actually don't want to become enlightened even though I say I do and am meditating regularly."* Some even say that they feel enlightened beings are holding themselves detached from ordinary people in some kind of an elite society, and they are angry at enlightened beings for being separate and elite.

In a more practical application of efforts, it would be a better use of our time to fearlessly contemplate our own attitudes toward the enlightened state, accept responsibility for any defective view, and begin fresh from where we are to change them. If our innate view and its companions of energetic influences on our mind are creating obstacles to our true and pure desire to attain enlightenment then we must make determination now to uncover the rascal hiding in our own mind!

Search for truth

How we develop strategies in seeking truth is influenced by criteria already present in our mind that we use as tools for this search. However, if they remain unexamined or we use faulty premises, we might arrive at ideas about truth and falsity that bear no relationship to reality. Contrary to some pop philosophies, there are actual realities and truths that need to be penetrated to evolve in the organic and natural method. We are gradually weaned away from false reasoning and eventually learn not to seek truth as another objective, such as having a fancy new way to personalize our life, feeling important by creating a new truth or just wanting to be different from everybody else in a faceless world.

Other criteria used for understanding truth are books of wisdom or even everyday wisdom sayings. I recently read about Benjamin Franklin and some of his writings. He also collected sayings of his time, about crops, the nature of people, trust, and other interesting topics he gathered into regular almanacs to guide others in everyday life. Aphorisms such as *"A penny saved is a penny earned,"* and other quotations range from folk wisdom to common sense reminders, and even things your grandma said that are still rolling around in the recesses of your memory waiting to be used.

Books of wisdom such as the Bible or the Pali Canon are still used as important resources for reading about true things. However, even holy books can be misunderstood and misused to harm others by applying personal agenda such as anger. On the other hand, if we observe positive changes in others because of their reading and thinking about what they found in books of wisdom such as religious scriptures, we can also be inspired and learn discrimination. As we read sacred books describing reality and practice new perceptions to train our minds, we become refreshed and reminded of our original nature of clarity and openness.

Lorig: Buddhist mind training

Although you may have an interest in spiritual subjects, it

is helpful to understand different kinds and levels of mind and how they are produced. To understand the nature of mind is to understand the root of happiness and suffering. The study of Lorig, the nature and functions of the mind, is introduced so that we become capable of discriminating between positive and negative states of mind and make strong determination to abandon negativity at the root, by our own decisions.

Normally, in the monastery, at least a year is spent studying Lorig everyday. Because I will be introducing a strong analytical technique later, based on Chandrakirtis analysis of Twenty Emptinesses, it is good to prepare for that by "warming up" our intellect correctly.

Although the various schools of Buddhism developed according to teaching lineages and many philosophical points of view, this is not the emphasis of Lorig. We could spend time looking at points of view or study who thought what and how that relates to another view but that might not be helpful. Lorig mind training is not the teaching of emptiness, not the teachings of healing techniques, or the Madhyamika Prasangika view. Therefore, I mention here what it is not. Any extensive teaching in Buddhism is defined by the parameters of what it is, and especially what it is not.

Foundational training in formal concepts is taught in Tibetan monasteries to all of those who are capable. The Abhidharma is only one of the traditional three baskets or collections of the teachings of Buddhism. Abhidharma is the largest collection; the philosophy, psychology, and commentaries on Buddhist views according to the method of each monastery or school. In that way, the various interpretations of the meanings are promulgated beyond general dissemination of important concepts.

The Vinaya is a compilation of scriptures on behavioral vows, ethics and morality. These are taught with the strict guidelines maintained since the time of the Buddha and all ordained are expected to know the meanings of the vows.

Sutras are direct quotations of Lord Buddha as best we can extrapolate from vast numbers of translations done over 2500 years. Many translations now come from previous translations, so much of Buddhist scholarship is based on refuting other translators' work.

However, we must receive all teachings with a Mahayana, or higher altruistic motivation, in order to maintain a correct inner focus without looking at our own ego. That is a correct viewpoint. Much more will be described later regarding Buddhist altruism.

Skillful doubt is easier than deluded doubt

So, we will explore a bit now about an aspect of Lorig; correct and incorrect doubt. A formal definition of doubt is a mental factor that vacillates with respect to its object. When the mind becomes mixed or associated with doubt, the mind itself, along with all other mental factors, such as emotions, motivation, and ability to distinguish between right and wrong, becomes blended with the qualities of doubt. In informal or everyday life, we may experience its effects, use it, or look at it, but we do not really analyze doubt itself, isn't that so?

Because we have to be very firm when practicing dharma to have confidence in the path and goal of our spiritual efforts, our mind must be free of wavering. Certain kinds of analytical meditation train us to observe two or more positions making dispassionate judgment regarding the correct view. That is not the vacillating mind-wavering kind of doubt.

When doing correct analytical meditation, we not only observe, but we also enter a stronger connection with the objects under analysis by deliberately dividing our attention between two or more viewpoints. An example of this might be thinking about karma or cause and effect as having either a positive influence or a negative influence on our behavior. This enjoyable type of meditation requires a great deal of previous inner work creating clarity of mind for best results. This will culminate in higher enthusiasm for dharma and an ability to resolve inner doubt so completely that eventually one becomes awakened in the manner of awakening achieved by Buddha Shakyamuni. Non-deluded doubt meditation practice actively seeks to resolve conflict by structured cogitation using correct logic based on healthy Buddhist principles.

However, improper doubt is a powerful reverse blessing. Deluded doubt not only shakes confidence and faith, but can actually cause one to stop spiritual practice completely should it get to a point where one cannot tolerate it. One can become discouraged by doubt. A lack of confidence, stamina and understanding needed for practice can cause the meditator to falter. That person's progress can either stop immediately or return into a tiny seed form. In this fall from being a practitioner, at best they revert to an earlier practice of mild interest but no longer sustain the enthusiasm of a practitioner.

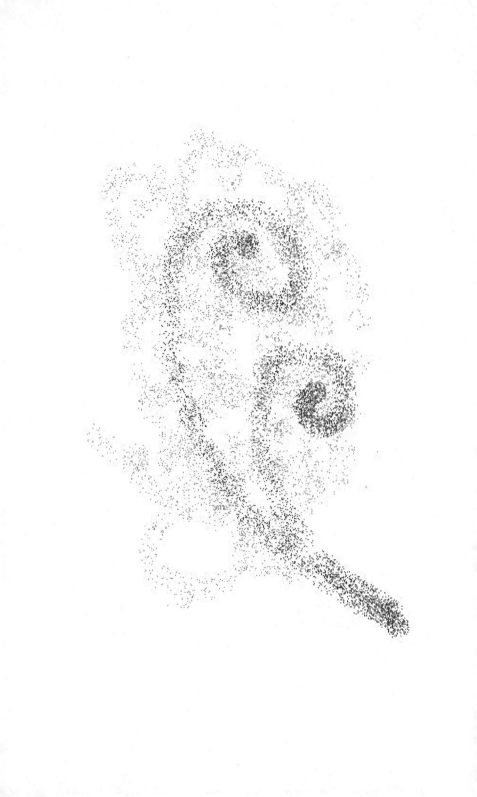

Chapter 2
Demystifying Emptiness
(Outer and inner based appearances)

"You might think that emptiness means nothingness, but it does not. Merely from reading it is difficult to identify and understand the object of negation, what Buddhist texts speak of as true establishment or inherent existence. But over a period of time, when you add your own investigations to the reading, the faultiness of our usual way of seeing things will become clearer and clearer"
His Holiness the Dalai Lama

We have an obligation to examine the elements of the human realm innate view and its relationship to the primary message of how we believe we are alive. However, in order to examine that in a meaningful way, we need to begin that discovery by demystifying the subject and dispelling the gripping anxiety that many people feel toward topics as scholarly as the Buddhist descriptions of the innate view.

Let us begin by remembering that an innate view would be, by definition, one that is not held by force of our will power. In other words, we cannot hang onto it by thinking about it because it is not held by intellect. It is also not possible to be held by recalling an innate view, either as *"These are the kinds of things that I believe in, me and my fellows,"* or trying to remember our innate view mechanically like a memory. Neither of these is called an innate view by definition. Therefore, it must be a hidden programming, adhered, or glued, to an inner mind such as the subtle subconscious mind and/or even more subtle minds that are still part of our mental continuum.

Buddhist sages and other early inner scientists discovered that we possess more than one subconscious or subtle conscious mind, which they have identified as inner, subtle minds. These inner minds have various kinds of veils or barriers that separate them from each other as well as from the outer conscious mind.

There are very specific energetic pathways toward higher development. Unlike walking into a lobby with many doors, there are not multiple doors opening from one main inner location for the purpose of our discussion of inner mind development toward the enlightened state. The structure of barriers and veils and how they work to hold space for higher development is a more secret topic. The important point here is that they do exist.

However, please note here that the increasingly subtle minds are only seen as subtle from a human realm perspective, not from the perspective of higher reality. The veils, barriers, and separations act to contain space for various levels of potential development and are presently like layers of plywood. In addition, if there is no development, these levels are pressed together. To an enlightened being, the appearance of this continuum array is according to the development of the individual observed. To a less developed person with limited inner vision looking at the inner minds of an undeveloped person, it does not have separations but an appearance like a steel plate preventing access to the interior. As the mind opens and subtle levels of mind begin to energize for awakening, the possibility for growth occurs within these subtle minds still correctly held apart from each other by barriers. Until then, that subtle mind has no self-awareness. In any case, since subtle minds generally do not hold human valuations such as methods of holding memories, they exist invisibly, even within more developed persons.

Subtle is stronger

It may seem that what is subtle is not very important as it is hardly here or discernible. In fact, the more subtle the inner mind, the stronger it is because it is closer to reality than the human tool of the functioning mind. From the observation by higher functioning and subtler reality, the increasingly dense and complicated ways of existing are identified as belonging to categories of living beings up to and including the human realm.

These are subjects of great concern to developed beings such as bodhisattvas and Buddhas. Their compassionate concern, and how that can become deliberate actions felt even in the dense realms such as the human realm, is the focus of many discussions. These discussions, in turn, find creative methods to help living beings become receptive to that care. The teachings of Buddhism such as scriptural advice, logical guidance such as Chandrakirtis "Twenty Emptinesses," formal commentary, as well as informal commentary, are all results of this compassionate concern in action.

In its most traditional form Buddhism states in a condensed way that the innate view is a confused or wrong view, that a self exists when it does not. That is not complicated. This overarching arisal or organizational principle called self is the object to be negated, as it seems to hold a function of binding elements without a function of its own. This conclusion reached by Buddhist thinkers, scholars, and observers regarding the need to destroy the foundations of this organizational principle by destroying our confidence in the self is repeated throughout Buddhist philosophy and psychological training in the Buddhist path.

Buddhist scholarly explanation of the innate view

The presentation regarding the innate view is held to be almost impossible to understand correctly. In fact, there is quite a lot of anxiety even among logicians and scholars to gain a correct intellectual view and understanding of the issues surrounding the innate view.

So, in order to prove my point, I will quote here a bit of commentary taken from classic Buddhist philosophy. "*According to this system, if one understands the mechanism through which all things are merely posited on the strength of conceptual thought, then one will easily recognize that any apprehension of an intrinsically existent reality is made in contradiction with this mechanism.*" This is actually very correct. If you memorize and repeat it, others will think you are very intelligent! They will say, "*I am not going to argue with that person because I have no idea what they are saying.*"

To continue the commentary, "*The person is nothing more than an imputation made in dependence on a composite of parts. Therefore, there is no other entity to act as the base. Every conventionally real thing posited by conceptual thought must fulfill its own function. This is a most profound subtlety of the Madhyamika view.*" If you wish, you can say form follows function, which appears to be a very modern concept, but actually, it is ancient Madhyamika.

Refutation of Buddhist scholarship by Western students

Since we need to address some of the concerns regarding the subject of the innate view most often reserved for scholars, I have asked some of my students to comment and below are some of their answers. Perhaps you agree, disagree, or have not given it much thought, which is probably where they are in their reasoning. Following their responses are more short passages regarding the correct Buddhist intellectually held view that is the reason the students are complaining. After that, I will present another model for understanding the view, although I am personally quite fond of the classic view presentation.

Student: *"What I hear Rinpoche saying here is that the argument is valid, but the analogy or language, the description that is used here, does not really resonate with us. I am saying that we do not think about things as wood and fire and water. We think about things as bones and blood or atoms and quarks."*

Student: *"We do believe that we are here as entities. We do believe it all the time. When you want to drink something, you think 'I want to drink something,' so, you believe in I, and so you take the glass and drink. If you did not believe in the existence of an I, then you would not have all those desires and all the negative emotions that come on the basis of this belief and ego, so it is present in all your actions and all your thoughts, and that is why we are in samsara."*

Student: *"Somewhere back in there, they said that they make this great point that a human is not conventionally real based on, and then you named five or six things, but in the West, we do not believe that anyway. That does not address our innate view of the modern person. It addresses the innate view of Indians 2,500 years ago. I could listen to it all day, and say, so what?"*

Student: *"Well, it is not the existence of the I and the negation of the I that I have difficulty with. It is using an argument that is so old, it is not pertinent to us."*

Rinpoche: Okay, these are some interesting observations, but let me go on with the classic Buddhist view worded so carefully and studied in this manner for scholars. *"Ultimately, even names themselves do not exist, and at the conventional level, there is nothing aside from that which is posited on the strength of these strictly conventional labels."* This is the main thing that is going to make you look good if you can memorize and tell it to others. You try to remember this part of the argument, okay?

"Because they are dependently imputed and dependently produced, none of them exists through their own intrinsic being. There is no independent entity not merely posited on the strength of some particular conventional label. The Svatantrika maintains that it is not possible for any epistemological object to be established in reality as ultimately true or in actuality, yet he does assert existence at the conventional level through its own essence, its own

unique distinguishing characteristic, and by virtue of its intrinsic being." Does that make it more palatable?

"*The absence in a living being of any base for qualification of this self is called the Selflessness of the Person, while the same with respect to the eye, ear, and all things is titled The Selflessness of Things.* All right, so at least now you know what subject is being discussed. "*On account of the apprehension of the psychophysical constituents as I, one goes on to imagine the existence of a self which does not in fact exist, and then he or she becomes strongly attached to this self as if it was ultimately real.*" Okay? This is the end of this quote. Now, we go back to everyday language here.

Two methods: Inner and outer based views of inquiry

So, what is the meaning of the innate view? Our interest in knowing the nature of reality is actually not because we are interested in reality or truth or anything related to those subjects. We want to be happy and we want to know more about me, our favorite subject. For that reason, like many people, after we feel reasonably satisfied and comfortable in life, we would like to enhance the quality of our life by knowing how and why we are alive. People who live in manifest suffering want liberation, but the intelligent, happy person wants to know what lies beyond. However, for those who are correctly satisfied, the vast unknown lies beyond personal satisfaction.

There are two distinct methods for understanding how we are alive in the world. One method is asking, "*Is there a self, or a state called selflessness?*" The other method is asking, "*How am I alive here?*" Of the two methods, the outer-based view is the correct classic Buddhist explanation of the unreality of human existence that chases the seeker of enlightenment with the stick of fear of the world as is described in the Pali Canon and Abhidharma psychology. It is a bad place! You should get out of it. You should transcend as quickly as you can because it is only suffering! Do not hang around here or even look back! This is the important outer-based view of the beginning stages of development and preparation for transformation by alerting us to the state of freedom away from suffering.

The runaway horse of the untamed mind

The purpose of the outer practices is to tame the mind. However, scattered training received by meditators might make them feel that the process toward enlightenment is like the untamed Wild West. They want to experience the sense of excitement, anticipation, and infinite possibilities in a wild rush toward the awakened state.

An untamed mind is like a horseman whose stirrup straps slipped. I saw in a movie where a rider slid underneath his horse; the horse was on top and the rider was on the underbelly of the horse, just barely hanging on, his head almost in the dirt. The reins were flying in the wind, and the horse went anywhere it chose. This is just like the untamed mind. However, the rider whose stirrups are tight is like one living in the vow to attain enlightenment. He is firmly seated on the upper part of the horse with the reins in his hands. This taming allows him to be the horseman and not the horse.

When the mind is untamed, mental energies are out of balance. When the mental energies become seriously out of balance, the mind is shaking, like the reins of the runaway horse. The mind is rising and falling like a sick dog about to heave. Like this, an extremely suffering mind is going up and down and is unable to deal with ordinary life, much less resonate with higher states of mind with undamaged energies.

Another poor method to tame our mind is to squash down mental energies. With some success, there could develop a lethargic behavior that might even appear as though the mind is tamed. Nevertheless, the moment an outer environmental issue arises, the original untamed energies can erupt like a volcano, producing anger or other delusions. Then it does not take long before the horseman is back underneath the horse, the harness all undone again.

A simpler method

The simpler method, in my opinion, is the inner-based point of view. All of vast life is happening interior to the gross manifestation of the human realm. The Tantras and scriptures describe in detail the existence of other realms or ways of being beyond the reach of ordinary beings.

The Buddha described his awakening from a dream and the state of release and relief that he experienced, free from the suffering view of the dream like state. We also have a large body of valid experiences described by other trusted sources, such as others who have awakened from the dream and escaped the oppression of the suffering view that takes the transitory stream of change to be solid and real.

Science is now maturing enough to be able to describe what authentic sources have been experiencing on the interior and describing for thousands of years. Both now agree that the way the world appears is not how it actually exists. Both now state that it is highly improbable that it exists at all, other than in a state of potentiality. In Buddhism, we call this potentiality perception and call this realm and other realms discrete perceptual realms. What science is not yet sure enough about is the interface between consciousness and its descriptions of physical potentiality at this point. As Buddhists, we are *"holding space"* and good wishes for those measurements to be done to their satisfaction as soon as possible.

Buddhist logical discernment

The definition of discernment is "the process by which two stimuli differing in some aspect are responded to differently." Deeper discernment is important to learn, remember, and put into practice. Buddhist logical studies and deeper meditation stimulate the actual inner practice, the only method to train the components of an inner alignment.

Energetic learning inside happens when the boundaries between deep theoretical possibilities of the human mind and the human subtle mind of the next interior level are stimulated and opened. Controlled discrimination is the method, and Buddhist logical studies, such as Chandrakirti's Twenty Emptinesses analysis of reality, should alert subtle minds that higher development training is desired. Inner discrimination and discernment in the ordinary mind, over time or lifetimes, becomes hardened, deadened, and distanced from inner senses and needs to be awakened.

The actual energetic discriminations prepare inner minds for the authentic inner senses that will arise after enlightenment.

This will produce a higher standard for later transformative work. More advanced work happens only in the subtle minds after they are trained, but in most human beings, inner minds are not yet activated. Therefore, what presently appears energetically to a subtle mind seems to be the same energetic dynamic, when in fact it is quite different.

Upon becoming alert, inner minds learn how to use discernment in the energetic form to prepare for transformation into another kind of being that would be literally blind and deaf if it did not have the ability to make careful distinctions between different kinds of stimuli. For example, your teacher in school probably showed you two words; "where" and "wear," and asked you what the difference was. In that way, the meditator will be expected to become receptive to discernment between two different stimuli that differ in some particular aspect and train in responding to them differently. That means making the correct energetic choices.

A facilitation by the intellectual mind is not the actual discrimination or discernment because the outer mind is not built to accommodate the inner concepts. It is important that we facilitate this process through mental functions such as cogitation, meditation, and logical analysis while allowing inner minds to do careful inner work. This method of using discrimination is simply the act or process of exhibiting keenness of insight and judgment based upon traditional Tibetan Buddhist values, while making quality discriminations or choices to gain the correct result.

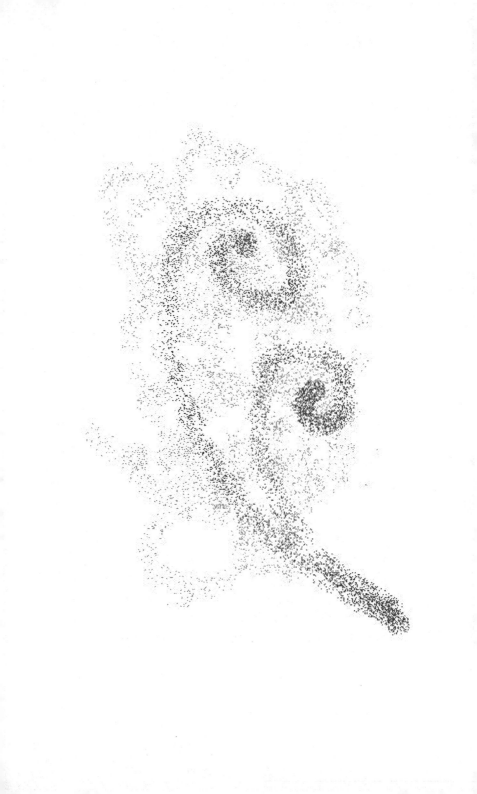

Chapter 3
The Real You (Who am I and what does that mean in reality?)

"One of the most important philosophical insights in Buddhism comes from what is known as the theory of emptiness. At its heart is the deep recognition that there is a fundamental disparity between the way we perceive the world, including our own experience in it, and the way things actually are. ... we tend to relate to the world and to ourselves as if these entities possessed self-enclosed, definable, discrete and enduring reality. For instance, if we examine our own conception of selfhood, we will find that we tend to believe in the presence of an essential core to our being, which characterizes our individuality and identity as a discrete ego, independent of the physical and mental elements that constitute our existence"

Dalai Lama (The Universe in a Single Atom)

All Buddhists pray to the inhabitants of the great realms of learning and progress such as the pure lands of the Buddhas and the bodhisattvas, requesting release from the suffering human realm experience, isn't that so? These realms are visualized in Tantric practice and are described so the meditator can make connections to the Buddha and guidance beings associated with the Great Path to perfection of that particular higher realm.

Enlightened beings that emanate into this world benefiting those living under the acknowledged imperfect conditions here encourage people to avoid believing in this world as a final destiny of evolution. As I have said earlier, science is now agreeing with Buddhism regarding the nature of physical reality within their own language. Science is now beginning an exploration of the important interface between consciousness and the illusory world of probabilities. For example, the erratic behavior of an electron stabilizes due to perception that gives it location; otherwise, it only remains as a probability. Buddhism, however, is already beyond that and teaches us how to explore the possibilities for preparation for transformation by the one living within an illusory realm.

You are not the one you think you are

Because this is a perceptual realm, the way you exist and the way you think you exist are different. I choose to call that misknowledge an aspect of a larger description of the innate view. Therefore, living in the illusory way means that you are not the one you think you are. In fact, you are not even alive in the way you think you are. Gross physical and gross mental functions possess an adhered innate view, and therefore, thinking functions are not perfectly reliable indicators or ultimate truth-determining devices even in very learned forms.

There is another kind of living being that is part of a more subtle version of the human being, alive on another level of reality, and that is the real you. You are not the real you. This living being is not a human being. It does not speak English, French, Tibetan or any known language. It is an energy- electrical being associated with the level of mind that transmigrates from its illusory lifetime to illusory lifetime. It was alive before you were born, and it will be alive when you depart from this world. This living being is already on an evolutionary journey to absolute perfection. This being is associated with the life process of the deepest inner mind development. Because it is beyond the need to enter into denser manifestation itself, it has emanated you, a perceptual form being, for important reasons.

Emanation is a natural process

Emanation, or gradual densification of subtle matter, is actually the same method by which the Buddhas, who are in higher development, emanate. However, this inner mind being, unlike a buddha, is not an enlightened being and requires bestowals and permissions to participate. It is self-referent, which means it only knows what it already knows, and it can only gather a certain amount of information based on its current level of confusion. This living being, whose present process has caused it to emanate into the human realm, has been emanating repeatedly into the human realm or other realms over a very long time. However, it has been delayed by confusion and forgotten that it needs to make transitional transformations to continue its journey.

This living being is the real you, or in any case, more real than you because it is more subtle, extremely long-lived, more comprehensive, and survives the gross death process. This extraordinary being appears to be internal to you, and by that, you might infer that it belongs to you, but it does not belong to you. You are its emanation. You continue to be connected to this being your whole life, and you belong to it.

The purpose of life

The nature of the inner being that is the real you inside is described so that we gain correct inner balance. This being is the real practitioner inside, the energetic alive being that is capable of attaining the transformation of enlightenment after considerable preparation. A dramatic and sudden change will cause it to transform energetically to another kind of being that also has a profound effect on its emanation being, the ordinary person. The process and these changes are described extensively in hidden language in the Tantras. This change also brings closure to its cycle of unaware lives in the human realm even though its emanated form will continue to live out a human existence. The dramatic transformation usually causes the person in the illusory human realm to wake up and become aware of their illusory nature. There should also occur a definitive break with the innate programming of the human realm.

Before that transmutation happens, you might wonder, if that inner one is the real you, then exactly who are you? What is your function? You should become a more careful caretaker and human facilitator of a sensitive process that includes enthusiasm for preparation to transform in your actual being. Therefore, within the parameters of the possibilities of transformation in this lifetime, there are elements of the innate view that are important for the caretaker/facilitator to discover and learn.

However, before the inner awakening of enlightenment, the ordinary person is not only bound by taking what is illusory to be real, but also holds the defective egoistic view that they are *the one*. To understanding that the inner life and actual being emanate and own the outer being, and not the other way around, often has the wonderful effect of resolving a logical incongruity.

This being is the real you that emanated into this human environment, but remains in a more subtle form, connected to you for the whole life, but distinct from the body and outer mind. Your actual being cannot be here in its present subtle form. In its earlier times, before human realm participation, this long-lived being completed much energetic learning. Preparation for closure from that earlier training place, that karmic realm, and that other way of being, required a *huge* effort. In other words, you were not always a human being. You have lived in many different forms and many different ways of being, but only by virtue of the actual real being and not you personally.

Energetic closure for fresh beginning

If the actual being completed energetic closure in some other universe or realm, it is unknown and unknowable if that was like enlightenment in that other way of being. Energetic closure has a barrier, as enlightenment does, and therefore, previous ways of being are generally impenetrable as memory. That energetic closure truly is a closing of a module of the journey. After enlightenment, actual being will not return to ordinary suffering human being. You will be connected to a different kind of being, an actual being that is an enlightened being from the viewpoint of the human realm, but still not from the viewpoint of perfection's care.

From the point of view of a previous existence of the actual being, the human realm might have been like a heaven realm or a pureland. Perhaps you prayed to the human realm, perhaps a far better place than before, to gain the human realm sphere. Your actual being then became an ordinary candidate for another way of being and received the permissions and bestowals that allowed it to emanate into the human realm for further growth and change according to the Great Path of Dharma. The path and dharma exist in many spheres or realms where living beings arise to experience the results of karma.

Receiving healing and bestowals

An important part of preparation is the energetic healing that needs to happen in the essence being, the actual being. That is why initiation is bestowed, in order to model the correct dynamics of a new way of being and to facilitate this change and healing in both the inner and outer being. It is also important in order to set in motion inner actions such as inner refuge and motivations such as desire to change that will produce beneficial results toward preparation for transformation. Outer refuge and maintaining vows of bodhichitta can be done by anyone, whether developed in his or her innermost being or not. The path is open to all and not just to the pure.

Student: *"You said earlier that when we are given the bestowals and become candidates for the human realm, there is a special kind of hypnosis that occurs with the actual being and also with this sense of a human being or this sense of self. Is the hypnosis of the perceptions broken from subtler to gross gradually, or does it happen all at once?"*

First, the bestowals are not given to you, but to the one interior, the subtle being. To imagine the innate programming as though it is given to the human being is not so useful.

That is because you are speaking through the filter of your innate view and still wish to be the one who is the actual alive one when that is not true.

From reality spheres of great compassion and guidance, such as pure lands and from Buddha fields accessed by quantum shifts in direction of our consciousness, help arrives, just as we prayed it would. By logic, these changes facilitated in us should, and usually do, come from the subtler toward the more gross. Nevertheless, a feature of existence of certain levels of development, such as higher buddhas, is the quality of being unlimited. This means that buddhas are capable of arising in any form, and so it is not necessarily from subtler to gross.

The cost of human life

Permissions to enter karmic perceptual realms are as certain as mathematical results and come at a price. The cost of that permission to participate is the innate view. The cost is displayed in a special dream-like, hypnotic state, in both the actual being and you, its emanation, in order to participate correctly in a new environment. The human realm is a perceptual realm. That means you are only alive here due to specialized, complex instructions filtered through a set of perceptions that are your personal gateway to live here as a human being. In our Tibetan system, we say a human being is nothing more than a mass of perceptions, but I say it differently here to give you some new ideas to think about. The fact that it is true should not hurt you.

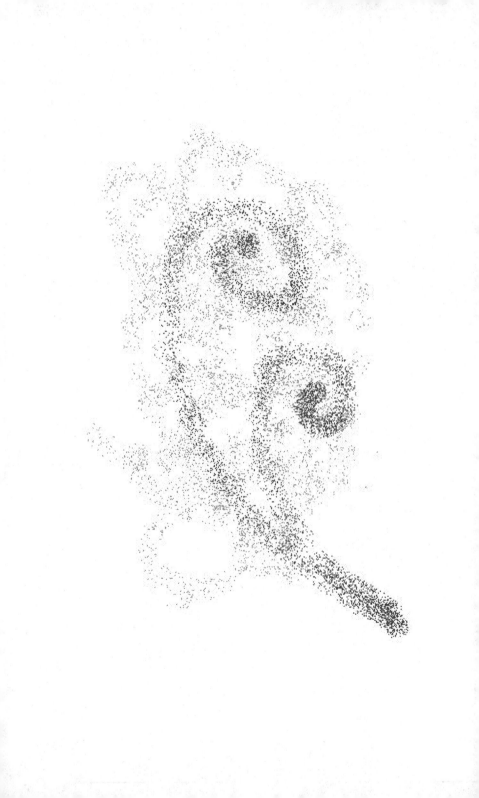

Chapter 4
The Hypnosis of the Innate View
(how it helps and how it harms)

"How much suffering and fear, and
How many harmful things are in existence?
If all arises from clinging to the "I",
What should I do with this great demon?"
Shantideva

The innate view that seems to be the primary cause of
suffering in the human realm is given too much credit for
its ability to make us suffer, in my opinion. This induced
dream has been, is now, and will continue to be created by
a mixture of causes and conditions, and we are living in
the karmically caused result. We seem to see karma as a
wrongness that others or we have perpetrated. This is not
true, of course, as the causes and conditions are both positive
and negative. The most basic distillation of the innate view,
according to Buddhist synthesizers, is the mistaken inner
and outer worldview that takes the transitory and illusory
to be real.

However, it is an error to indoctrinate people with a view
that everything is bad and wrong due to primal ignorance of
true nature, but to encourage them to rejoice in appreciation
of human life if they are actually in preparation and not

just because they are human. The preparation process will require a closer examination of the innate view to gain a better outlook of seemingly contradictory understandings of primal ignorance and appreciation.

Encoding of the innate view is the unconscious price paid for participation in the human realm. This compassionate imprinting is without regard for the reason we need to be here or are forced to be here. Because the human realm is a specific place, not an example realm or a dream realm, the programming is specific to this realm. Because of this, many aspects of this programming are unique to human life. It will do you little or no good in a later transformed state, and will be discarded at the time of transformation.

During the lifetime or in order to enter the human realm, the individual must be naturally connected, for example, by previous karma, or a connection must be induced by design. An ordinary being is an example of the former; an emanation bodhisattva, an enlightened spiritual hero, is an example of the latter.

Our world view

Karmic beings need to be weaned away from an addiction to the programming by becoming mature enough to create a new world view. This comes alive by the strength of an emerging sense of universal responsibility, the heart of the Mahayana, the great vehicle of altruistic meaning and actions. It does not matter if the causes within the individual are positive or negative if they have created an uncontrolled cyclic series of arrivals in the human realm. In other words, we are bound by the attachment to the programming, and within that, become fascinated by the display of virtue or non-virtue.

The elements of the innate view do not define or demand how the individual worldview is experienced and therefore cannot be a cause of the suffering of confusion created by inappropriate use of the innate view. To prematurely destroy the foundation of the programming without changing first is an act of desperation of the manifestly suffering person wishing to escape the results of their confusion. A traditional view to escape the dysfunctional human state is strong in Buddhist practice and meditation, so study of the workings of the ordinary and the evolving mind is unavoidable if we wish to become free from suffering. The preparation for transformation needs to be done gradually by addressing the dysfunctional energetic display that continues to make that being a candidate for the human process. It would not be beneficial to make them unsuitable for human life without preparation for a proper future environment. This is why the lower Nirvanas are not places of permanent salvation, but more on that later.

Buddha means Awakened One, and the process is literally one of awakening from the dream-like programming to a new alert state called enlightenment. The first stage of enlightenment, as a minimum standard, is achieved when one knows without a doubt that the perceptual knot that holds the dream-like state to be authentic is not real.

Five aspects of the innate view

Now we can describe some of the points of the programming that are addressed in preparing an individual who is ready to enter higher training.

1 - A perceived separation

There is a strong perceived separation from others that actually does not exist in the perfected state. Through the innate programming, the individual is caused to be unaware that, at the core level of their actual being, he or she is perfection in order to make efforts to evolve in the natural and organic perceptual awakening to complete balance. This is not just a feature of the human realm innate view, but is common to all views in all realms. However, in the higher realms, the sense of separation is less than what is experienced in the human realm.

2 - Confidence of solidity

There are different levels and perceptions of solidity that are perceived in the human realm. Naturally, we feel the pull of gravity and the physical consequences of our universe of quantum mechanics in its usual manner. However, there is another kind of solidity felt even in the physical body unrelated to gravity or even lack of gravity. The inner energy of the world relates to our inner energies in continuous communication that gives us a sense of solidity. This further gives rise to a kind of confidence and safety feeling that a structure holds us. Otherwise, we would feel like we were floating.

Within this structure, we perform actions and enter into dynamics with other beings that also experience a similar sense of solidity. This is a correct connection. However, in dream states, many will experience release from this and float, move instantaneously, fly or experience other sensations while partially disconnected from the innate view. This sense can also be experienced during meditation and actually acts to prepare the meditator in an organic and natural method for a careful and confident transmutation to another way of being.

3 - Hypnotic blinders

There are hypnotic blinders placed on the human mental faculties that prevent us from being alive to vast interior where life is actually experienced and the life force of the human individual resides. Creating aversion to arise if the blinders are approached by instilling fear appears to be a terrible thing to do. If the meditator is careful and does not return to ordinary mind, thinking they have found the goal, they will then experience the event of enlightenment or awakening effortlessly.

4 - Simplified parameters

The innate view allows the individual to collect information within a simplified system that is linear. This allows beings to perform actions with enough time to make non spontaneous decisions and use an emerging sense of careful will power according to their values developed by experience and changes already stabilized. These actions come from and result in exhaustion of appearances that are connected and related to levels of inner minds that are incapable of using will power or discrimination by their structure and nature. A correct application of mental functions uses the inner energetic life force while creating energetic nutrition for inner levels by manipulating ideas created by inner and outer events combined with memories still within the innate view, now done more skillfully.

The physical body already has a sophisticated nervous

system, part of which acts as a bridge to more subtle minds that can be affected by actions beyond the use intended by the imprint of the innate view. For example, the limbic system can hold trauma by being imprinted and programmed with shock to the nervous system. These effects are not part of the innate view and must be healed so the memories held there are not of distress and confusion, but a kind of new knowing in the form of remembering. In the abuse of the innate view, actions of karma further bind and solidify an individual to a confused sense of identity that actually does not exist except as a consequence of misuse of the innate programming.

5 - Projecting perceptions on others

The deepest level of our individual development over a very long time is the actual being that has emanated into the human realm in order to make important changes for further development in the perceptual journey to perfection facilitated by correct illusory change. The inner being is partially active and accessed in the human realm to imbue objects and others with awareness in order to interact and even to see them. This is connected to a primary function of human existence. For example, if I am looking at Jinpa across the room, I cannot see Jinpa unless I see *me* in Jinpa. After the first moment, I do not actually see Jinpa anymore; I only see me. This is a ramification of the first point, the induced sense of separation, a function of the innate view.

An important activity of projection in the human realm is to seek closeness, perhaps as a consolation for separateness. For example, a girl and boy fall in love and want to see and be with each other. However, only at that very first moment before they are even aware that they have seen each other, do they actually see each other, or in the Buddhist terminology, experience bare perception. In the second moment and thereafter, they only see themselves in the other. This is followed by interaction with their own projected perception and memory of the first moment.

How the innate view damages our evolutionary development

How is the innate view preventing you from being and living right now in a pure land such as heaven or in some Buddha field? The answer is both complicated and very simple depending on the stage of development of the individual. It is simple because the innate view is deceptive and false for someone close to transformation. The inner signs of impending transmutation inside then become more real than how the world appears. If the meditator is careful and does not return to ordinary mind thinking, they have found the goal, they will then experience the event of enlightenment or awakening effortlessly.

On the other hand, evolutionary transformation is complicated for someone enmeshed in karma and its consequences, compelling suffering rebirths. This one is unable to gain enough freedom to think clearly. Confusion regarding how we are alive can divert our precious life toward goals and desires based on cyclic continuity of births, and we might make decisions that will perpetuate that. Furthermore, the suffering person will develop likes and dislikes based on confusions and develop trivial as well as deep obstacles to transformation, leading to the unhappy result that they cannot understand the preparation instructions for transformation when they are offered.

Forgetting or losing the instructions

These issues are among the traditional problems associated with learning our True Nature. Another problem is forgetting the instructions. Sadly, there are many people so enmeshed in many kinds of suffering that not only do they not understand the instructions, but they do not have an opportunity to receive these important preparation instructions for transformation. Involved in everyday life and trapped in the machinery of their own karmic events, they are not even exposed to the path of preparation. If they do come into contact, because of obscurations or poor development, it is meaningless to them. Poor development can also mean following a path that is not liberating. For example, some work very hard to become powerful and gain the ability to control many that will have damaging results. This definitely shows how the innate view can exacerbate harm to evolutionary development by seeing others and the self as separate and unequal.

A student recently questioned, *"I understand Rinpoche, that if the innate view is held in our perceptions, we hold the perceptions of a human being. But if we held the perceptions of being located in the pure land, in fact we would be in the pure land."*

It could be so, but that is not necessarily true. On one level of your being, you could have an intellectually held perception of existing in a pure land, this is even practiced in the tantric path, but energetically you could be nowhere near actually being a candidate for existing in a pure land. Instead, the location of your actual being could be the energetic equivalent of some drunken bar. If it is not ready to be alive in a higher form, that means it is not prepared.

Nice dharma becoming dry or solidified

Another way that harm occurs is when the innate view becomes too mixed with the teachings of dharma or religion and becomes focused on stylized, dry rituals and dogma. In this way, the cure can become a further disfigured dynamic. The very pathways for the healing cure and release can then become a cause for further confusion or suffering. There is also a strong possibility that the individual may become disappointed in learning about higher spiritual life and end up believing in nothing.

As we continue to discover how the innate view aids damage, we notice that the innate programming could become overly strong, too solidified and with too great a sense of separation. These ramifications are unhealthy and cause the individual to lose the natural ability of the lightness of flexible mind to accept the vast understandings of the path to perfection.

Instead, the guiding and sheltering care, in the form of permissions to participate in human life, should be viewed and used as a delicate employment of principles. "By the power of compassion;" this is how the reincarnate lamas and other awakened benefit beings see their existence in this world. It then becomes like a ballet, a dance, or a theatrical play.

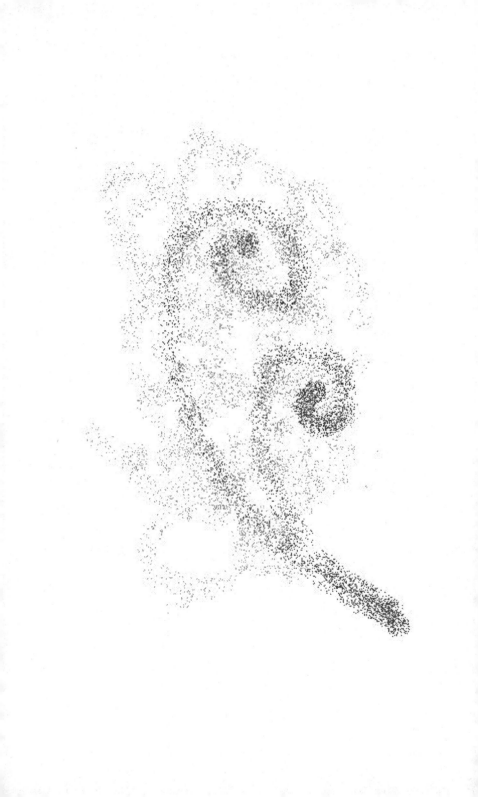

Chapter 5
Buddhism and the Ego
(self-cherishing and the higher yogas)

"Sometimes, the thought of 'I' suddenly arises with great force.... like that of a rock or a tree seen protruding up from the peak of a hill on the horizon. Likewise, the solid 'I' which seems to exist somewhere within the body and mind is merely an imputation. The body and mind are no more represented by the sense of 'I' than is the protruding rock represented by the word 'human.' This 'I' cannot be located anywhere within any individual piece of the body and mind, nor is it found within the body and mind as a collection, nor is there a place outside of these ...

The Second Dalai Lama (1475-1542),
Samuel Bercholz's *Entering the Stream*

Using practical efforts to help others transform to the enlightened state, Buddhism sometimes changes into a system that attempts to erode the superstructure of the ego. This does not work as well as it should because the punishment of the ego will usually cause it to submerge, change or adapt to the harsh methods used to destroy it. You actually cannot crush the ego. The mind is very tricky and changeable, and so it remains in spite of efforts to destroy it. However, it can very easily morph into a disgusting display of impoverished self-degradation that is totally fake. It is scary to watch a person attempt to control their ego by hiding self-cherishing in humility. They can even be hiding it from themselves.

The ego is suffering and needs to be separated from the overactive, over-stimulated, and unaligned energetic state of confusion. The self-cherishing that is a feature of unenlightened existence, as well as inappropriate pride, need to be destroyed in order for one to be rescued from the suffering, imprisoned state. The ego, a kind of organizational principle, needs to be healthy, flexible, and strong enough to withstand and flow with the rigors for preparation for transformation. The beaten down ego is useless!

The end of self-cherishing

Self-cherishing that holds I, me and mine as supreme receivers of all benefit and relates all events from that central position is gradually replaced by greater and greater concern for others. This is due to the systematic training of the Mahayana, the awakening of altruistic compassion.

As a practitioner becomes more aligned toward their next stage of development, the veils and barriers that hold them into a particular view of solidity begin to erode. The meditator begins to have experiences of previously unseen forms, flashes of colors, feelings, as well as energetic movements that do not seem to relate to the human experience. The gradual adaptation to an expanded view is accomplished in meditation and not by becoming fascinated with these awarenesses as psychic powers to be used.

The innate view that classic Buddhist philosophy describes

as taking the unreal to be real also takes the more subtle to be unreal. It functions as a set of blinders to the myriad forms of unseen life surrounding the individual. This is another ramification of the simplified parameters of the hypnotic programming called the innate view.

The need for a mentor

"Rely on the teachings to evaluate a guru:
Do not have blind faith, but also no blind criticism."
His Holiness the Dalai Lama

When the innate view is beginning to erode, that person very much needs a mentor to explain and to introduce the perceptual orientation from a new viewpoint. The transitionally transformed being that the human practitioner is becoming inside also needs to keep a good balance while they are gaining new understandings. The changes that they are experiencing are part of a natural and organic process of transformation.

The natural process of evolutionary development is facilitated and guided outside by the enlightened mentor who has already been through the process. From the interior, where the Great Path continues, guidance developed by perfection itself in its compassion form of enlightened beings, such as deity and inner and outer mentor, will help the meditator as much as possible.

How the innate view helps evolutionary development

The innate view helps us by imprinting deliberately simplified parameters. Perhaps you think human life is complex, but it is not! We actually live in a simple world, a very simple world. Deliberately simplified parameters allow the person in preparation for transformation another way to learn small and careful lessons without distraction. That is why highly evolved practitioners seek to be reborn in the human realm.

There are yogic practices specially developed for human practitioners who pass away before they complete the training they need for enlightenment. These practices allow them to be reborn here either by karma or strong wishes to be reborn as a human being granted by their mentors, deity and Buddha to gain proficiency in skills they need for the next phase of their development without needing to start over from the beginning of development in each life!

The completion stage practices of the advanced meditator require lifetimes to perfect and will be the direct cause for their rebirth and subsequent activities benefiting others as part of that practice. Many of you are struggling with daily practice in early stages of becoming competent, and yet even now, you can appreciate the value of the human realm if you find the cultivated methods and teachings to continue practicing the inner yogas.

These special inner yogic practices are for future stages of development. Important practices that inner yogic beings need to accomplish here in the human realm include preparation for actual perfection-based compassion to arise after enlightenment.

We learn compassion by stages

Do you think that this compassion is going to be experienced before enlightenment? That is not possible. However, if preparation is done carefully, the actual compassion arises after enlightenment and requires further training. This actual compassion arises in order to prepare the new bodhisattva for entry into the enlightened society of benefit beings. This higher functioning community needs the newly awakened ones to become capable of getting along with many different kinds of beings in order to benefit their own process to perfection. Right now, most human beings cannot even get along with themselves, much less myriad beings existing in other forms.

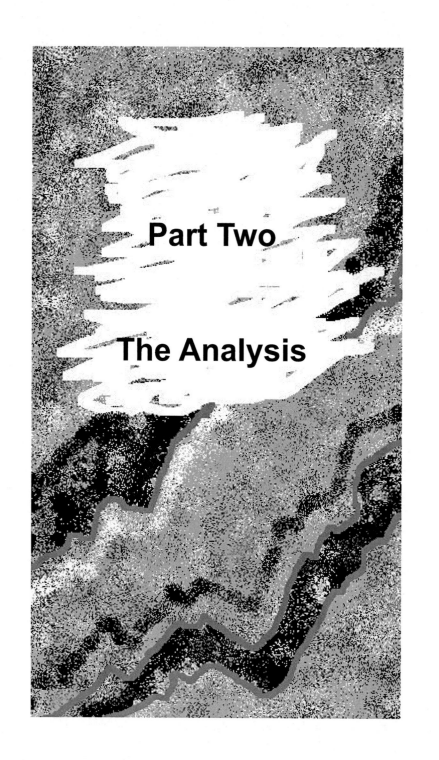

Part Two

The Analysis

Chapter 6
Faith in Logic

"Love is the seed of this abundant harvest of buddhahood.
It is like the water which causes growth and expansion,
And it ripens into the state of lasting enjoyment,
Therefore at the outset I shall praise compassion!"
~ Chandrakirti

When we learn about something complicated, we need scientific methods, medical diagrams or business terminology to act as matrices to hold new concepts. The study of the nature of reality has used philosophical language since early times to support non-physical data in a more or less scientific approach where theoretical boundaries are the norm. However, standardized logical calculations, formulas such as tetralemas and even mathematical logic are used to challenge at its core the profound illogic that prevents people from experiencing reality. The challenge to the intelligent is to root out the illogical and force it to enter into a new dynamic with outer and inner mind relationships based on valid methods. Because we are not alive in the way we think we are, it is an absolute necessity to deny our present view in favor of one that is more aligned with a higher reality than self-referent human intelligence.

Cultivated faith and trust

In Buddhism, there is a cultivated faith in the Buddha and other great beings such as Nagarjuna and Chandrakirti, who admired the Buddha and were later admired and studied by other great masters such as Je Tsongkhapa, among others. The faith of these masters, combined with the faith of your own teacher toward these extraordinary teachers, should create in you a sense of trust. These earlier guides were skilled in thwarting the intelligent, ordinary, evolved human being away from destruction by error.

Ordinary human evolutionary development has produced certain excellences, and inventors build upon the work that has been done by others. For example, people do not reinvent the computer in order to improve it; they build upon the knowledge of others. They learn standards and baseline operations of technology in order to hone their skills. In other words, they have a certain well-placed faith in what has already been accomplished by others. Pressing the start button becomes an unconscious act of faith in what has already been invented and described. In that way, if you are a software or hardware developer, you add your faith to your work by using tools already there.

A potential problem arises, however, when errors become compounded by trust in what has been decided before. In a way, evolution of ordinary human intellect has always been bound by how things were "always done this way" or how advancement has been accomplished in the past. There is even an enhancement of pride involved in setting in motion the usual, tried and true "creative" pathways that eventually prevents even the most intelligent people from arriving at radical new higher development, whether in medicine, technology or philosophy.

In the process of learning, people rely on logical truisms that must be accepted in order for them to become intelligent, successful human beings. However, many previously accepted truisms are now disrespected as thinking inside the box or inside the envelope, as the saying goes. Now, creativity demands new tools when ordinary tools do not work; in other words, fresh thinking outside the envelope. So, we already have a dynamic within our culture that disrespects the usual, ordinary, even intelligent strategies for being able to understand how the world works.

Destruction of error

Now we can go back and add that interesting dynamic to the cultivated trust that we must have and develop even more. Rather than deny existence entirely or reject all trust and teachings, we instead quietly observe the self-anarchy demonstrated by the Buddha when he blew up his own ordinary mind with the bomb of special analysis. This analysis was based on thinking outside the envelope, but still contains all of the factors of reliance that come from encouragement from guidance. Nagarjuna blew himself up, and Chandrakirti also blew himself up. Je Tsonkhapa blew himself up. You might say, *"Well, if it worked so well for so many people by blowing themselves up, maybe it is a good idea to try it myself."*

Each of these intelligent people has been able to overcome the defects of their ordinary, evolved intellectual mind and turn away from certain destruction by the error of common faith in ordinary development which infected them like a virus. That is what I mean by the destruction by error.

They would have been destroyed had they not been able to overcome ordinary intelligent mind. One must succeed in destruction *of* error or succumb to eventual destruction *by* error.

There is a big problem with the application of strategies by the evolved intellect toward understanding the nature of ultimate reality. These strategies, however intelligent or complex, do not have the slightest possibility of creating personal affirmation of reality. This possibility does not exist because that exact intellectual, evolved position is intimately related to the human realm perceptual support, in other words, the innate view. This is the innate view from which you suffer, so you cannot rely on that which brings you suffering as a support to understand the nature of reality; there must be another way.

Agenda

Although most philosophers and all scientists say that they are objective, lines of inquiry often begin with a strong agenda or premise that they are trying to prove. If they cannot prove it, they let it go, and if they can prove it, it becomes filled with additional data from their own agenda. Do they want to draw you into a perceptual position, such as the great nihilist, Nietsche, that is hopeless because nothing exists? Is that what they want you to believe? Well, that is not very nice. To bring additional despair into the world would not be a good agenda.

In order to overcome the conditioning that holds us to suffering, we need to understand how we are alive so we can become free. The human innate view is a part of a perceptual story bonded to your essence being to help you be alive in this realm. If you do not have an innate view, you are not here!

Emptiness and Nagarjuna

Emptiness refers to the lack of intrinsic reality of all phenomena, and love is a state that seems to depend upon ordinary human reality to exist. We embark now upon an inquiry into the mystery of how these two could possibly be connected. In order to reach quality conclusions regarding their potential relationship, we will need to explore the traditional Buddhist meanings of emptiness, although I believe my commentary does diverge into more original thinking than many I have read. Chandrakirti's exposition of the twenty forms of emptiness will give us a good foundation in classic Buddhist thought regarding emptiness.

I have concerns about insipid commentaries by people who supposedly have studied Buddhist scripture enough to teach, but actually do not seem to have that strong a hold on their own view of emptiness. One unnamed Tibetan lama, after each verse of powerful commentary by Chandrakirti states, *"It's empty, Lord Buddha said it's empty, and therefore it's empty."*

I have no qualms or argument that Lord Buddha Shakyamuni did in fact say these things. I truly believe that this lama's message was that, because we have great faith in the words of Lord Buddha Shakyamuni, and because he said it, it is so; that is that! That was good enough for him, and I hope it is good enough for others, but in case it is not sufficient for you, let us look at it again.

We should also make effort to correct the connection between the annoying dryness of many scholars' statements and the actual juiciness of the subject. This dryness should not spread any further than the halls of the dry pride of intellectual understanding of the nature of emptiness. Abuse of knowledge should go no further. Let us, instead, learn this philosophy based in bodhichitta, the wish to attain enlightenment so that we can be of benefit to all sentient beings. That is the only way I am actually interested in discussing it.

Nagarjuna and Chandrakirti
The holy father and son

Chandrakirti was an abbot of Nalendra, or Nalanda University, the greatest and largest Indian Buddhist learning center. The Madhyamika middle way philosophy, or more specifically Madhyamika Prasangika, also known as the Consequentialist or Dialecticist school, is associated with the original teachings of Nagarjuna.

Chandrakirti's text, *Madhyamakavatara*, on the Middle Way position regarding the nature of reality provided a more understandable and expanded interpretation of Nagarjuna's (c.150-250 CE.) view. This eloquent commentary is now used as the essential study guide of most Tibetan monasteries in their studies of emptiness, or shunyata, and Madhyamika philosophy

Nagarjuna, a Buddhist who developed the philosophy called the Middle Way, lived approximately 1800 years ago. He did not develop the structure of logical debate known as non-affirming argument (in other words, not this and not that). This was already a common form of logical analysis alive in Hindu philosophy even before Nagarjuna, but he used it so well that it has perhaps become more associated with Buddhism than Hinduism.

Nagarjuna's important contributions

Nagarjuna's important work is *Mūlamadhyamakakārika* in Sanskrit, or in English, *Fundamental Verses of the Middle Way*. Our discussion here is based on Chandrakirti's *Entrance to the Middle Way*, the clarification of that earlier work by Nagarjuna.

There are other books that you might see in your local library that are translations of Nagarjuna such as *Seventy Verses on Emptinesses*. Another text I appreciate very much is called *The End of Disputes*. I also like the next one, which is called *Pulverising the Categories*. It sounds quite violent, and I believe that he intended it to be so. Then there is *Sixty Verses on Reasoning* and *The Hymn to the Absolute Reality*. I am just giving you some titles that may strike you as familiar, that you may have seen, or perhaps you have them high on your library bookshelves in a kind of reverential position.

A student once told me, *"Rinpoche, I realized that I purchased the first book you listed and with great enthusiasm took it home, and at some point I put it on the shelf. One day I took it off, opened it up and looked through it a little bit, then reverently closed the book, touched it to my head, and put it back on the shelf because the blessing was about all I could get from it."* Like that, perhaps we are just reviewing your library contents. Another commentary is *Constituents of Dependent Arising*.

Your aunties' old needlepoint

There are many Buddhist scholarly works, and the fact that Nagarjuna's works have been worthy of preserving should demonstrate their value. However, for some people without a good grounding in basic principles of logic, reading and trying to ascribe value would be a bit like having an estate sale of your great-great auntie's goods. As the family looks through auntie's objects, one or another family member calls out, *"Well, this thing is no use, but this, now this is beautiful. Let's hang onto this,"* and it is placed on the knick knack shelf in their house. Perhaps another auntie put another one on her shelf, and when she passed away at her estate sale, others saw and exclaimed, *"Oh, these things are not my taste or fashion or worth anything. Throw them out."*

You know, at estate sales, you often see the artistic efforts of elderly ladies, from knitting impractical baby clothes to painting wooden spoons with sayings on them to crafting things from kitchen towels that are hard to understand. I have watched wonderful old ladies, who should properly be making cookies for all of us, instead making cross stitch or needle point squares so they can cover up nasty, naked boxes of Kleenex. Some have designs of teddy bears or little flowers or some pretty color.

It appears that, to some the rule is, under no circumstances should there be anything in a proper home not covered with plastic needlepoint. Meanwhile husbands are busy too, making similar artistic creations, bird houses out of milk bottles or Coke bottles, and other amazing artifacts.

Some might question, "*What makes something worth holding onto beyond sentimental value? What are the qualities of objects that hold value generation after generation? What short list of things avoid being discarded and are worth preserving for thousands of years?*" There are only a few artistic creations and precious remnants of antiquity in written form that have survived destruction thus far and possess enough value so that we wish to continue to hold them dear.

However, if we never study the classics or struggle to understand Nagarjuna's thoughts, but instead put them on our shelves and hold them as objects of veneration, we have preserved them for nothing at all. Perhaps we are thinking that we would not want to wear them out by looking at them.

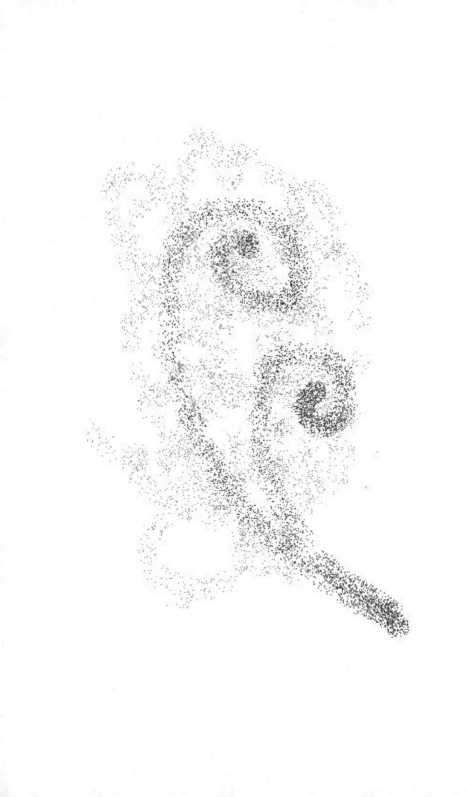

Chapter 7
Learning Reality

"Therefore, Sariputra, in emptiness there is no form, nor feeling, nor perception, nor impulse, nor consciousness; No eye, ear, nose, tongue, body, mind; No forms, sounds, smells, tastes, touchables or objects of mind; No sight-organ element, and so forth, until we come to: No mind-consciousness element; There is no ignorance, no extinction of ignorance, and so forth, until we come to: There is no decay and death, no extinction of decay and death. There is no suffering, no origination, no stopping, no path. There is no cognition, no attainment and non-attainment."

The Heart Sutra

The innate view is part of a perceptual story bonded to a living being such as a human being, as well as connected to a particular subtle inner mind. The innate view, or taking what is transitory and impermanent to be permanent, is reinforced by society along with our own experiences of the world as solid and unchanging. This complex set of instructions is bonded to the living being in order to help it be alive in this perceptual realm. You are only alive here by your perceptions. If you do not have an innate view, you are not here! You will continue to be alive via the innate view until the correct view replaces it.

Even the inner bases, the more subtle minds that hold various relationships to human life and inner life, are illusory, as they are even more fully hypnotized into taking the transitory to be real, and rightly so! You would not be here to have this wonderful opportunity as a human being unless you were capable of receiving the various cascading effects toward the gross mind while holding the innate view.

To have an innate view does not mean that we are bad people or that we did something wrong and are being punished. The innate view is not evil. For the one who is in preparation for transformation, it is simply not needed anymore because it is time for the ordinary mind to evolve. For the one in preparation for transformation, to continue using ordinary mind and its structural support, the innate view, would be like wearing a very old winter coat that does not keep you warm anymore. It is getting threadbare, looks shabby, and the very thing it was supposed to do, it cannot.

Beings such as bodhisattvas who emanate into the human realm because they have work to do uproot the innate view that delivered them here so that they can begin careful activity to benefit living beings. All beings seeking liberation from the sufferings of uncontrolled rebirth and misalignment with reality must also uproot the innate view. We say that the destruction of the innate view occurs with arising the correct view, but there are important transitional correct views for the benefit of bodhisattva trainees. There are trainings for bodhisattvas in stages according to their development. This training allows for skillful transformation from the initial stage of understanding the nature of human existence to eventual establishment in complete and total Buddhahood. It is definitely a step-by-step process even after one becomes enlightened.

However, we do not damage the perceptual programming by rigid logical analysis too soon without first developing transitional correct views in order to be able to recognize the correct view when it arises. It is not possible to add a correct view of reality to a contaminated view. The transitional correct views must include training in compassion practices, understanding karma and reincarnation, overcoming fear of death and how to rely on virtuous objects such as the Buddha, dharma and sangha. When the Great Path of the teachings is intergrated into one's mind so seamlessly that there is no difference between the teachings and the mind, that one is considered to be a candidate for higher training such as intense introduction to emptiness.

Point one
Emptiness of the inner:

"Since it has no inherent nature, the eye is empty of being an eye. The ear, nose, tongue, body, and mind are the same way. They are all described in a similar way. They are not stable nor forever lasting, nor do they remain for a short time and decay. The eye and the rest that are the six inner ones are things that have no essential nature at all. This is what is meant by "emptiness of the inner."

Chandrakirti

Even the inner bases of the outer senses, such as the ear of the ear, et cetera, are illusory arisals, as they are even more fully hypnotized into the belief taking the transitory to be real. We are talking about the inner eye of the eye and more subtle to that, up to consciousness itself. Each of these bases lacks the marks and signs of actual reality. In addition, they are an inferior kind of learning device and should be seen for the poor quality dynamics that they are, particularly in comparison to new dynamics being presented. They exist as part of the structure receiving the programming for human manifestation. We do not attempt to directly reprogram inner minds from the outside except by the reproducible foundational concepts. Otherwise, we could damage the mind.

We have been fooled, beyond the carefully balanced innate view we need to participate in the human realm, into thinking that the inner bases have spirituality, holiness or will provide something that they are not capable of providing. Therefore, we should not blame our innate view, although in most philosophies and practices, this is exactly what is done. Perhaps we should begin to disrespect it cautiously because our actual dilemma is not the fault of the innate view. The innate view has allowed us to participate in this human realm for a very long time, but once we began to think that it could provide us something that it cannot, we were wrong.

The correct view

An analysis such as Chandrakirti's Twenty Emptinesses is meant to deliver us to a perceptual position where there is no place to rest our innate view. That is why it is called destruction of error. The innate view will dissolve naturally with analysis in deep meditation, without loss of energetic integrity, and will be replaced by the correct view, but only with proper preparation. Then the innate view will be dismantled, and the correct view arises. If it is done right, the correct energetic configuration results and is called the correct view. The real value of the correct view is that it allows one to continue to maintain the powerful inner connection with reality while still being able to participate in the human realm with an adjusted view. The correct view is a valuable conventional awareness of balanced wisdom arising in the human. It is also the staging location of a transitional view for what happens next in development.

Inner bases

Since even the more fluid inner bases are illusory, they are also fully hypnotized into believing the transitory is real, yet some believe these inner bases to be the evolutionary, intellectual, evolved structures with the highest capacity to discover the nature of reality. Different kinds of bases, not just inner sensory bases which emanate the gross outer sense bases such as gross consciousness, but various inner minds, are also illusory. They lack the marks and signs of reality and are inferior kinds of learning devices that have helped to create and reinforce the self-referent nature of the activities of inner and outer mind. The inner minds should be seen for the poor quality dynamics that they are, and we should begin to rely on authentic bases, such as what is presented to the inner as acceptable principles. This is unique to the individual in preparing for transformation. Thus far, we have been fooled into thinking there is something in the mind that will provide something that it is not capable of providing.

Even the inner bases of inner minds lack the very element that we expect to be the support of our inquiry into the nature of reality. Eventually, all avenues of inquiry will be exhausted in this diatribe against our illogic. When the mind releases its grasp correctly, there will be an inner practice alive and an opening of a deeper inner mind. This then signals a readiness to move into a kind of vestibule where there will be a washing of latent impressions and stains of the innate ordinary view. While this is happening in the interior, the practitioner has yet to create perceptions that can be used without the crutch of the inferior view.

Reality and falling asleep in meditation

The practitioner has not yet created new perceptions regarding how things actually exist and must therefore continue to rely on the crutch of the inferior view. Students often say, *"I am doing my practice, and boom, I suddenly fall asleep."* This happens because they do not yet hold an organized structure in their perceptual continuum where new knowledge, new perceptions, and learning can rest and stabilize. Therefore, they cannot stabilize what is being presented. This is actually very common.

The reason why you receive teachings is to help create new perceptions. Inner teachings arriving to the ordinary mind prepared by knowledge and practice recreate the mind so that someday you might instead say, *"Wow, I can now understand something that I could not understand before."* The new perception on the outside helps us, so when the teaching comes from the inside, we connect with it. Otherwise, we do not understand and become the weakest link of our own inner process, unable to support or interpret the knowledge offered.

Sometimes inner teachings come in the form of bliss or in the form of sensations and feelings. If it is intellectual knowledge that we need in order to have a careful outer process and we are not stable in that, we may simply fall asleep suddenly. Another reason that we might fall asleep is that, in the very place where this new healthy perception is arriving, we are just so full of our own intellectual certainty that when the correct perception comes, there is no place to put it; because we are already full of ourself! Therefore, we fall asleep. However, do not give up at this point because something good is actually happening! Keep working on meditation, listen to teachings, and put them into practice to become increasingly capable.

I reiterate, while this is happening on the interior, the practitioner still has not created perceptions that can be used without the crutch of the inferior view that continues to take what is transitory and illusory to be real. They do not have the perceptions yet to support conscious existence in a new way, yet the crutch of their ordinary view is useless! The inner teachings cannot be processed, so they enter into a lower level state without foundation, which is sleep, whereas a more advanced practitioner would remain quietly alert. It is not complicated. Many try to make the emptiness search into some kind of exciting and exotic Las Vegas circus of philosophy when it is very simple.

This state without foundation is not a permanent state, but a preparation for still another condition to arise. During the experience of that new condition, it is usual to feel that you do not know if you are awake or not awake. You do not know anything at all, and later you will only remember that everything that you thought was the support was not there, and therefore we call it "empty." Since there are many kinds of empty, this state is important because it can happen early in practice, and many have experienced it and felt confused. It is an important state because it shakes our faith in the reality of the world and the validity of our cherished worldview.

Point two
Emptiness of the outer:

"For these reasons, form's nature is emptiness;
Therefore form is empty of being form. Sounds, odors,
things that are tasted, and what the body feels too, all
these phenomena are exactly the same. Form and so
forth have no essential nature: This very lack of essence
is called 'emptiness of the outer.'"

Chandrakirti

Chandrakirti, in the exposition of the Twenty Emptinesses, declares the emptiness of the subject, which refers to dharmas or heaps of accumulated manifestations belonging to the subject or to the appearances of forms. He states that from a human point of view, all phenomena, whether a personal body or the mountain ranges, are similar in their lack of deep inner validity. Very briefly, this is what Chandrakirti is telling us, which was quite wonderful. However, if you do not understand yet, I will add to his thoughts.

We do not need to accept or refute whether the eye, the ear, or other sense organs are co-processing centers of the senses. We already understand that the brain processes incoming data in ways that make it suitable for mental events and constructs such as personality to be created. That these fleshy sense organs and the fleshy organ of the brain are not reliable transmitters of data is already well understood by science and can also be demonstrated in personal observation and experience.

These organs can be damaged by disease, function with poor genetic makeup such as congenital poor eyesight, and can be easily fooled, such as seeing a snake when it is a rope, isn't that so? If there are people witnessing a car accident, there can be five people with five different experiences of what happened. The senses can be easily fooled and err often.

The actual outer and inner organs of perception are in the mind and not in the brain. They are not located in the physical body, but in energetic form invisible to human sight. In other words, no matter how you cut open the human body seeking the whole makeup of the senses, you cannot find the inner bases of the senses or the actual mind. You only find the fleshy brain processing neural signals that come from the mind. Can you tell where the body ends and the mind begins? No, they are connected by a spectrum that includes the manifested physical form. The brain itself can be stimulated, but it does not have consciousness itself.

Therefore, the physical senses are empty of what is perceived as their purpose without the connection to the actual inner sense organs of the mind. The inner sense bases are also dependent on another dynamic from even subtler mind that influences them. This means that events from the inner and outer environments continue to be processed through an inferior filter that is easily polluted, in other words, the contaminated senses.

"A consciousness that conceives of inherent existence does not have a valid foundation. A wise consciousness, grounded in reality, understands that living beings and other phenomena—minds, bodies, buildings, and so forth—do not inherently exist. This is the wisdom of emptiness. Understanding reality exactly opposite to the misconception of inherent existence, wisdom gradually overcomes ignorance"

His Holiness the Dalai Lama

Reality, self- cherishing, and misplaced hope

The very thing that we have hoped and relied upon to be real and stable and act as a support for meaning is in fact without the very thing that makes it seem real to us. Now, I have to state it in another way because it is important. That which you have relied upon does not even have the possibility of creating this support because your current view belongs to the human realm perceptual support, in other words, the innate view. What you rest your hopes on to understand reality is the illusory innate view that is not meant to support or perceive the very thing that you intellectually want it to. It is not possible for the innate view to do this. It is only the perceptual story that is bonded to your essence being to help you be alive in this realm, nothing more, and nothing less.

Delusional self-cherishing, by harming others in favor of our own selfish needs, causes the innate view to become damaged and distant from its original purpose. Correct self-cherishing has an important function of self-protection that allows us not just to be here, but also to continue being here. If we did not have certain kinds of protective self-cherishing, we would not be able to endure the psychological and physical onslaughts of human life, as our inner beings are far too sensitive. Buddhism helps us reduce and eventually eliminate the harmful aspects of self-cherishing carefully by presenting us with a better option of cherishing others. If you simply lost self-cherishing, you would be fragile and helpless in the onslaught of ordinary life. At the first opportunity, you would give up, so part of the correct view discussed earlier needs to be a more balanced sense of self-preservation. Mentors often feel concern for the eating habits and daily physical care of someone who is freshly in the correct view because much of their self-cherishing has been destroyed.

The dangers of self-cherishing by misusing the ego or other sense structures inappropriately are extensively covered under other teachings by myself and others. Even the ramifications or secondary effects of self-cherishing have caused you or others to do so many things for which you were later sorry. Now that we are discussing deep subjects here, your responsibilities increase to reduce poor strategies of self-cherishing.

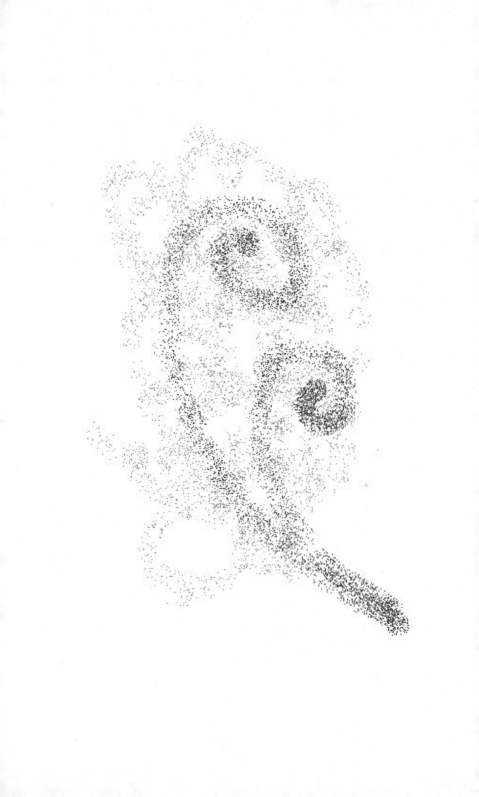

Chapter 8
Reality and the Dreamlike World

*Remember too that the victorious Buddhas have
recommended in countless open and secret scriptures
that we seek the correct view of emptiness, the one that
absolutely destroys every tendency to grasp to indications
as objects themselves. This then allows us to avoid the two
extremes of thinking either that things exist independently,
or that--if they don't exist independently—
they cannot exist at all.*
Je Tsongkapa, founder of the Tibetan Geluk tradition

Continuing the discussion point two of Emptiness of the
outer by Chandrakirti, our intention here is to develop the
desire to enter into a certain state without foundation. The
purpose of the analysis is to compel us to seek something
that, upon specialized reflection, we cannot prove is
actually there. In that way, the mind will release grasping,
but maintain a direction, a specific trajectory that allows us
to arrive in a correct view. Chandrakirti declares emptiness
of the outer, saying, *"For these reasons, form's nature is
emptiness. Therefore, form is empty of being form."*

We can do mental exercises to achieve a state without
foundation even though it happens naturally in highest yoga
tantra deity practices. We do the exercises because we need
to participate more fully in the transformative process in

various methods at various times to gain the full result. What is being addressed in Tantric practices emphasizes a different dynamic than this mental analysis. We want to become skillful on all levels of our being, even the outer gross mental level of body/mind.

This analysis should be done with prepared faith in the Buddha, Dharma, the teachings, and the enlightened body of practitioners, the sangha. When done with this special faith in a reproducible and blessed method, we will not arouse or experience unreasoning fear. Through analysis, we will become familiar with conceptual components, such as overcoming the fear of death through logic and study of interdependent origination. We can then understand better what is happening when new thoughts and inner experiences come. Meditators who could benefit from the analysis can become frightened, rigid or put off by study about emptiness, thinking, "*Oh, that is for scholars. I am just a simple practitioner. I will just do my practice, and that is good enough.*"

There is a famous Lam Rim story about Je Tsongkhapa, who founded the Geluk tradition of Tibetan Buddhism 500 years ago. He was teaching these or similar instructions on the nature of reality to a large group of monks and noticed that one of the monks was grasping onto his own collar. Je Tsongkhapa said, "*I see that so-and-so has discovered his own innate view.*" The monk was trying to hang on because, as his innate view was dissolving, he could not find himself anywhere. There are many benefits from receiving inner and outer teachings with a qualified mentor that stimulate correct reasoning and encourage the exposure of the individual view.

Form's nature is emptiness

Continuing on, Chandrakirti states that form's actual nature is emptiness. Therefore, form is empty because it has the manifestation of form. In addition, pleasant, neutral or unpleasant sounds, odors, substances that are tasted, and body sensations such as a breeze on your face or arm, a headache or tingling in the toes; all of these phenomena are exactly the same in that they do not possess intrinsic permanence. Furthermore, form cannot arise and remain for even the smallest fraction of time because it is illusory. This very lack of essence to satisfy our grasping is described as emptiness of the outer.

To awakened beings, even those awakened ones who still have a human body and mind, worlds and their contents exist as dream objects. All worlds are dreamlike, and this human perceptual world is not a particularly scary one. It is a regular old, standard-issue perceptual world. It is like a dream object. It should not be relied upon as the excellent support for superior meaning, as it was never intended to be so.

In manifestation, everything that has form cannot exist in that way unless it is empty of essence. Nothing that has form can exist as form unless it is naturally empty of the very essence that might prove its existence as it appears to ordinary mind. That is just how it works. 'Hmmm', you might think. 'Hmm.. why.. why... ahhh! This means'... And rightly so.

Form is without the inherent essence we perceive with the innate view filtering our worldview. The core that mind craves as a support, as real and true, is in fact like a dream object. We must keep our mind going in the correct direction so that the trajectory will take us to the correct view and a correct conventional view of the world. Therefore, we focus attention on emptiness of the outer to gain the correct understanding.

It is proper to separate and single out the various elements of our current view of reality to expose and further weaken our own illogic. We already looked at the analysis of emptiness of the inner, so it is not indicated to mix these two points together to create a synthesis. We continue to separate the strands of our illogic in this way because the innate view depends on the fact that we do not examine our own view correctly or with the motivation to benefit countless living beings. The Mahayana motivation of altruism brings a new power to the analysis that overcomes the feeling that we need to protect our view.

Reality and that nameless thing

The very thing that mind holding the innate view is trying to sit upon as the excellent support of its inquiry into valid cognition does not exist. That thing does not have a name. It is not called tree, or body or self. It has no actual name, but it is something that you innately believe is there, though it is not! Therefore, everything that appears as form cannot actually exist as form unless it is empty of essence. It is not the fault of form that it cannot provide the actual deep support that you energetically crave. Even more subtle forms that surround you, such as smoke, odors and the sounds and impressions brought through the senses by food, and your interactions with it by tasting, are all equally unreliable as the excellent support of your craving for stability.

Some people wish to substitute the word matter instead of the word form, although form encompasses more than physical matter. This is probably because matter, quite recently in fact, is not found to be the solid substance we sense it is. Even the underlying quantum levels of energy are not as we thought the foundation for matter would be. However, whether you choose scientifically described composition or analytical description, the same conclusion will be reached; matter is not a suitable support and, in fact, is carefully unsuitable for supporting the grasping mind. No wonder beings are suffering. No wonder we are suffering.

Point three
Emptiness of the inner and the outer:

"That both inner and outer lack an essential nature is what is called emptiness of the inner and the outer."

Chandrakirti.

If we move our awareness from outer forms and outer sensations and then believe that our thoughts and inner mental events are real, we are again mistaken. The shift in awareness from outer to inner "realities" can create a sense of pseudo authenticity of its own, and we may feel we have a superior reference point to check the validity of perceptions. This can cause us to gain confidence that we now have a good method of grasping what is real.

However, as a byproduct, this shift might cause us to feel that mind is an unsuitable location for reality to arise because the inner senses are dulled and damaged from abuse over lifetimes and unskillful activities that have created confusion and distress. In that case, we might choose to take specially empowered outer forms such as Buddha statues or political systems or the solidity of a piece of rock crystal to be a real and steady support, at which point we are even more misguided.

Further, some say, *"I only believe what I can touch and feel!"* Another one says, *"Everything out there is a dream, but inside I am real!"* Neither of these is correct, and neither is the skillful method to leave the suffering state of confusion and understand what is truly real. Point three of twenty emptinesses states that everything, everything, both inside you and outside you, is exactly the same, meaning it is without essence coming from its own side and neither creates nor displays reality. Now we gently but firmly pay closer attention because we are chasing our innate view hither and thither without blaming it or distressing our minds. We do it calmly and carefully!

Point four
Emptiness of emptiness:

> *"All phenomena lack essential nature, and the wisest of those call it emptiness. Furthermore, the wise one, the Buddha, said, 'This emptiness is empty of being an inherently existent emptiness.'"*
>
> Chandrakirti

A lack of intrinsic reality of what is named emptiness is the emptiness of emptiness. The Buddha taught this way to counteract the mind's tendency to solidify and think of emptiness as something that is truly existent. Chandrakirti and Lord Buddha Shakyamuni are describing what I call a state without foundation. This new term is used in order to increase your understanding by presenting a fresh point of view rather than saying the same thing repeatedly.

At this point in the analysis, the freed up energy, released from its bond to the innate view, is beginning to cause grasping so great that the inquirer will strongly want to hold onto something real. This is a prime reason why many who are capable of finishing the careful analysis stop here and grasp at the various levels of possibilities in a synthesis that still uses the innate view too strongly. We see how the great religions, new age thinking, or individual spiritual journeys form around one or another level of manifestation, claiming it to be the really real. This can stop the entire process of carefully dismantling the innate view.

Up to this point, we have intellectually understood that everything is emptiness without remainder, and now we intellectually know from what it is made. It is made out of emptiness. Unfortunately, emptiness has become something real at this point for the analyst. This is due to the pressure on the innate view programming trying to readjust to new parameters, grasping toward the next potential focus for its craving. This emptiness grows in importance and becomes a really real something. However, even emptiness cannot be the excellent support of your craving.

Point five
Emptiness of the great:

"The great is what the ten directions encompass,
all sentient beings and the entire universe. The
immeasurables prove the directions' infiniteness. They
pervade the limitless directions, so they cannot be

measured in extent. That all ten directions in their
completely vast extent are empty of essence is the
emptiness of the great. The Buddha taught about its
emptiness to reverse our concept of the vast as being real."

Chandrakirti

For the educated modern person, shock is a normal reaction
to learning that all inner and outer events, forms, sense bases,
and even trust and reliance on emptiness are not what you
feel you were promised in the search for truth. This could
have the effect, then, of driving your awareness to seek
refuge in the undifferentiated magnitude of living beings,
because you believe they are real in their combined life
force. That means that you might believe all sentient beings
as an aggregate possess something real. You might gain a
sense of personal safety by thinking; '*We are all one and that
feels real.*' This is the experience of universal oneness that
is the basis and goal of many spiritual traditions. It is also a
stage of growth where many kind and well meaning people
rest in their compassion and inner identity without delving
any further. However, this is not any form of permanent
liberation from suffering, but only a temporary respite from
the rigors and suffering of individuality.

The cosmos

The mind might change again and wish to look to outer
space, the constellations, the vast systems of stars and
planets and possible life on other planets as the vast reality.
One might see oneself as just a speck in that vastness. This
is a natural reaction after feeling self-important and finding
that identity to be without essence. Diving into a small place
within a vast cosmos might feel like a correct relationship to
vast reality. However, this vast is of the very same baseless

nature as the grain of sand and is not the excellent support of your craving.

At this point, you might also feel that your cultivated sense of emerging bodhichitta is threatened and has little or no value. Your present investment and cultivated faith in universal responsibility, at this point in the analysis and at all points in practice, should be the alive and vibrant wish to save all sentient beings. Now that wish needs to be reintroduced and attached to the corrected view. This corrected view of the altruistic wish to be of benefit to all sentient beings must be coupled with a careful intellectual understanding of the illusory nature of the world in order to mature.

Point six
Emptiness of the ultimate:

"Because it is wanderer's supreme of all needs, nirvana's cessation is the ultimate here. Nirvana, the truth body, is empty of itself, and this is what the emptiness of the ultimate is. The knower of the ultimate taught the emptiness of the ultimate to counteract the mind's tendency to think that nirvana is a thing."

Chandrakirti

Now, after rightly becoming disappointed with the vast as a flimsy excuse for true reality, the seeker makes great effort to acquire something real that makes sense. The meditator is then encouraged to embark upon the path that is common to all seekers of cessation, to remove the thorn of craving forever. With this aim, he or she begins to withdraw the mind from sense objects, rejecting the world of ideas and mental constructs and developing an even stronger wish to enter into another way of being that is actually truly real. This extreme step seems to be the last option to become free of the suffering of craving.

However, the meditator still holds a distorted view toward a goal that has the same defective problem that all other phenomena have: the perceiver is inappropriately grasping toward it to receive from it a solidity that it does not possess. This is because, and only because, the bonds of the innate view are still holding the practitioner into a model that is dependent upon the human valuation of freedom and is not yet prepared enough to step away from the protective cover of the innate view.

Reality and heaven

Even the heaven realms, the pure realms and holy places of pilgrimage that practitioners look to as the excellent support for their craving and grasping, are empty of essence. Devotees of this sort are looking for a special kind of spiritual good within ordinary stability, one that will support them in their life process and make them feel secure and virtuous. However, the dynamic they seek from these holy realms cannot fully satisfy them because these realms do not possess the qualities that the devotee ascribes to them in a solidified spiritual manner.

How can living beings have the correct view while still grasping and craving toward something that it cannot provide? I have explained it. Chandrakirti said this too, and Nagarjuna told him. He just explained a bit more. Nagarjuna is telling you what the Buddha said; we all say the same thing with a determination and validity. A valid meditation practice is based upon the understanding that the innate view is still in place and that you are in error. Have I or have any of your mentors given you any indication that an innate view is the excellent support of the deeper practices? Never. You will become a much better meditator when you release the grasping at your innate view.

Some will object, saying, *"Didn't you want my innate view to mature by attaching it to aspects of my meditation practice, the Buddha, and grasp after the practice? Now you are saying that is wrong? But you have always told us to turn away from grasping and grasp onto the virtuous? Wouldn't it be better to say as a result of this analysis, 'Well, everything is empty, so why bother to do meditation practice?'"* Yes, that would be an error. That would be a big error, although many people have done that. They say, *"What difference does it make? Everything is empty anyway!"*

Another tactic used is reasoning, *"Even though it is called empty of intrinsic reality, would it be okay to hold onto this little bit of meditation process as being real? Now Rinpoche is telling me it is not okay to hold onto even this, and that does not seem fair."* I answer that your belief in it did not make it any more real to begin with. However, I do love the enthusiasm of your process, and so we are looking at it in the correct way.

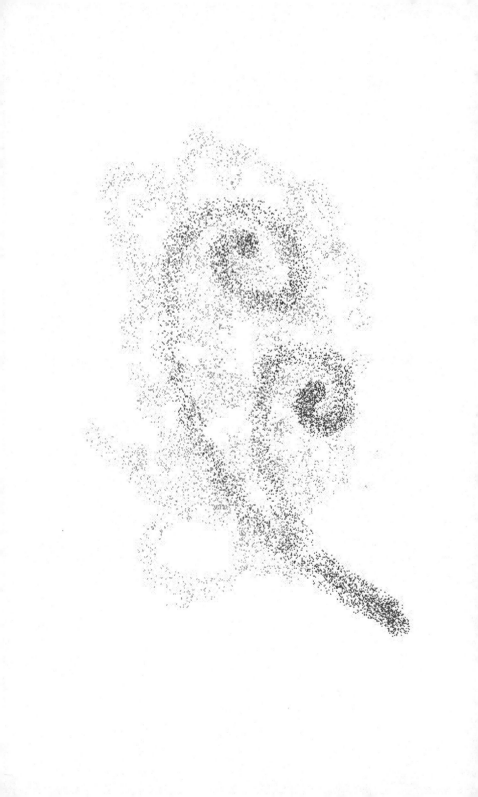

Chapter 9
Reality and the Grid of Manifestation

"I am not, I will not be.
I have not, I will not have.
This frightens all children,
And kills fear in the wise"

Nagarjuna

Point seven
Emptiness of the composite:

"Because they arise from conditions, the three realms are composite, it is taught. They are empty of themselves, and this, the Buddha taught, is the emptiness of the composite."

Chandrakirti

All realms where living beings exist are held together in a complex structure created and based on the needs of their inhabitants. Realms of humans, gods and lower beings, as well as the animal, hungry ghost and hell realms, arise from causes and conditions that facilitate their manifestation from energetic grid models interior to their outer manifestation.

In previous teachings on how to be more effective doing world peace prayers, as well as teachings regarding how the world actually exists, I have explained how energetic grids act as transitional supports for vibrational manifestation.

Our particular realm has a certain kind of energetic grid that is a pre-manifestation, or subtler energetic version, of the human realm that we recognize as the ordinary world we live in. In the same way, in other realms, other structures operate as the support for the different kind of manifestation of that particular perceptual realm. Because everything that has form is actually empty of self-existence from its own side, it is possible for this grid to arise due to the needs of beings with karma to experience certain kinds of effects, thereby providing an environment commensurate with those needs. This energetic substrate, or grid, exists for many beings simultaneously because it is a close match for any individual who corresponds in their interior individual grid and karmic needs to what can be provided in a particular realm.

Causes and conditions ripen in the individual, exacerbated by previous confusions, virtuous self-cherishing actions, and non-virtuous self-cherishing actions that have inappropriately dragged the innate view deeply into their interior mind where it does not belong. This produces a certain kind of disfigurement in the transmigrating living being that will match the parameters to enter this world. However, it does not mean that they are the same as the grid; they become a candidate for arising in manifestation in that realm. As I have said before, living beings cannot control this process.

In Buddhism, we say that beings are attracted toward manifestation in one realm or another by karma. It is not something that we spend a lot of time on other than the explanation of the between life state called the bardo. Saying that living beings are attracted to a particular realm means there is a special kind of desire toward an object that is being activated. When we say attracted toward in English language, it usually means a liking toward, but that is not true here. Living beings cannot help this attraction and therefore helplessly arise in form in a particular realm. Therefore, living beings arise from the results of the very causes and conditions that facilitate spontaneous manifestation from disfigured grid models in their own interiors.

Death and rebirth

Meanwhile, the Tibetan lamas were busily trying to help those who had passed away from physical life. We worked to clean up the living beings recently in human form and change them, to make them unrecognizable for entry into the lower realms. We tried to remove the causes and conditions the best we could. I myself was very active in this procedure to change the karma of living beings who had passed. Now I see it differently, but that is another subject.

There are many new age ideas presented as reasons for being born here as a human being. Meeting with soul mates again or choosing one's own rebirth in some cosmic conference are a couple of ideas in other philosophies. However, it is unusual for an unenlightened person to have deliberate relationships that transcend lifetimes with another specific ordinary person. To have such a relationship implies that you have choices, and that is what you do not have. This is the suffering of uncontrolled rebirth, being impelled or compelled to take rebirth in one or another suffering realm separated from loved ones. Our karma remains with our self and is perpetrated on others or our self without regard for individual connections. In general, the connections with others in this life are example effects of other times and situations ripening and presenting themselves for opportunity for healing once again.

Repairing karmic damage

At this point, the evolution toward the correct view might change again with another good idea arising to repair all of the broken promises made in previous lives without concern for who performed actions toward whom. Once we have gained a more comprehensive understanding of karma, the deeper, unresolved energetic wounds of karma within the continuum of the individual need to be addressed. The careful meditator desires to repair all the damage caused by previous lives experienced as unhappy karma in this life. We believe we are going to fix it up perfectly so we can leave this suffering realm. This is very good reasoning.

However, while you are trying to fix it, what else will you muddle? Who else's toe will you step on? Karma cannot be exhausted through karma. It is true that virtuous karma produces an easier life. It is also true that non-virtuous karma produces more suffering for yourself, others and unfortunate repercussions beyond that, but karma in general will never release you. You cannot become virtuous enough to be released through karma.

For most of you, your present situation is that you are an adult and have had experiences that have changed you. You have come into contact with others and have continued in this life to produce causes and conditions that will ripen in the future. You are now the product, not of the causes and conditions present at your birth, but those of your present day. Many meditators wish to remember their happy childhood in comparison to their own stressed present lives. *"How could I have made my life so complicated when it seemed all so simple and easy to think about spiritual things when I was a child? I knew there was something I had to do in this life that was important. Why don't I just go back to that feeling of simplicity and stop reinventing myself into what has caused me to be here in the unhappy, unsatisfied way I am right now?"* However, you cannot go back. You are already different from that child due to life's experiences. The actual healing must come from another method.

Interior grids of manifestation

Therefore, consider that the present day interior grid model where you arise and fall away simultaneously in your interior also comes from causes and conditions. These interior grids of the various realms also come from causes and conditions. Remember, we are still on point seven here, regarding the composition of realms.

These vast grids, which are the pre-manifestation of the three realms and the myriad realms, as well as the individual grids in harmony with these realm grids from which arises the individual, all come from causes and conditions. Because they come from causes, they are empty of essence from their own side and not capable of intrinsic, self-arising support of form. They are not the excellent support your cravings are seeking.

Reality and the cosmos

I feel a strong sense of sharing in this commentary about the analysis of reality and wish for many to benefit in the future by your understanding. The statements by the ancient Indian Buddhist sage Chandrakirti and my commentary are systematic methods to bring the meditator correctly and easily to where the mind has no place to settle in the dysfunctional view.

We now go on to ideas that frequently arise at this point in the method. Mind is seeking solidity and comfort. This could be expressed as a wish to say, "*Well, if I do not exist, then I feel a sense of safety that the cosmos and the great constellations exist. I guess I do not care if I do not exist as long as that exists and I am okay just being an illusory speck within that cosmos. If that is the way it is, then that is the way it is.*"

Chandrakirti says, and I echo him, "No!" The cosmos and all of the stars, even the Hubble telescope, do not exist in reality from their own side, have permanence, or exist at all other than as illusory, interdependent and temporary manifestations. Even the delightful images that the Hubble space telescope transmits back to us in evanescent digital form are empty of inherent existence, as are the starry objects that they captured.

One might say, "*Well, if that does not exist as you are telling me, then okay. I accept that everything in the human realm and all the things that I experience are illusory, but I bet there is some place that I have not discovered, and that does exist. Maybe some pureland actually exists, and that is real.*"

Therefore, before we lose our dharma practice completely, we again stabilize the mind. Yes, the Tibetan singing bowl I have in front of me IS here. Yes, I can ring the bowl, it is here, and the sound is here, but just not in the way we presently think it is! We are addressing that error by gaining objectivity and familiarity with the workings of the innate view as it tries to perceive reality, producing a correct intellectual view. From its own side, the bowl does not have inherent existence, but comes from illusory intention and materials. This bowl and the sound it makes both arise from causes and conditions, but because we are suffering from magical thinking we need to wake up to the way things actually exist! That is why they call the Buddha the Awakened One. The Buddha and myriad great awakened ones are no longer hypnotized.

"Moreover, when the extreme of existence is dispelled by appearance and the extreme of non-existence is dispelled by emptiness and when you know how emptiness is perceived as cause and effect, you will not be captivated by extreme views."

Je Tsongkhapa

Ordinary siddhas of magic

As meditators become more focused and energized, due to causes and conditions, there could arise what is called ordinary siddhas, ordinary super abilities such as unlocking a door with the mind by looking at it, seeing the future or hearing at a distance. These will arise either spontaneously or after having deliberately done yogic practices and visualizations. In fact, the ordinary siddhas could arise without that person being enlightened. That is why they are called ordinary siddhas because they do not display signs of enlightenment itself. If the meditator becomes fascinated with ordinary siddhas, their advanced studies will become diminished, and their attention and energy will be channeled into the siddhas. This will likely recreate them into a seeker of power that will eventually harm many.

Siddhas are part of a line of development that you already have with the dear ones in your family. For example, you do not want to tell them directly to pick up their dirty socks, and so you might say to them mentally, '*Now you come here. You Want to Pick Up Your Socks. You Want to Pick Up Your Socks.*' Then one day they miraculously pick up their socks. However, it is uncertain if you had the "super power" because, chances are, you had done this a hundred times with no effect whatsoever.

Joking aside, should you become obsessed with using techniques with others, eventually you will become like an ordinary magician and will continue to accumulate karma. In this scenario, one will often think that they are no longer affected by karma and may create suffering and discord through carelessness.

Previous training

There are valuable practice realms such as the human realm, so we do not disregard or consider useless our meditation practices, such as visualizations, healing and helping living beings. Correctly done, these will create authentic siddhas in you, in the future, in other realms, after having accomplished your training in the human realm. Do not disrespect the training that you are recieving or doubt that, in the future, training you have accomplished in the human realm will arise to save you or another being. There are beneficial activities that you will be permitted to do. Now, what realms have you existed in, and what kinds of training have you received in other places that you might presently be using for amusement or money making because of self cherishing? To me, it makes good sense to caution at this point in the analysis.

Abilities, the vestiges of previous trainings, are certainly unusual by the standards of the human realm. However, in other ways of being, in other times or other perceptual realms that you may have lived in, this was simply the training that you received. Perhaps you even accomplished the meditations and achieved signs of success that made you a candidate for the completion of that training.

There is no intention here to present a system that requires diagrams describing where realms exist or how many yogyanas they might be located underneath the earth. This discussion is about larger principles. For me, the specific curiosities are boring. When people ask me a question about details of esoteric knowledge, I feel like I just want to fall asleep. I am not trying to be bored, but sometimes I struggle to be interested and may have nothing to say, so I am sorry. However, be informed that what I say about boring subjects might just be something social and may not come from wisdom.

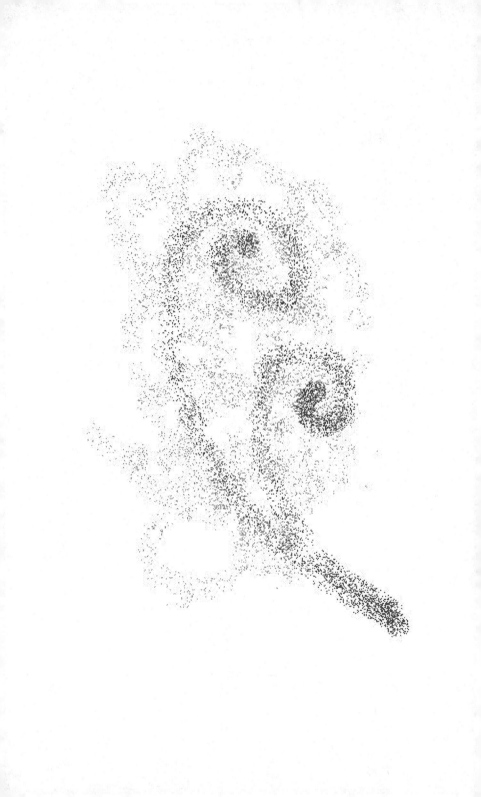

Chapter 10
Reality and God

*"Far away, in the heavenly abode of the
great god Indra, there is a wonderful net
which has been hung by some cunning
artificer in such a manner that it stretches
out infinitely in all directions. In accordance
with the extravagant tastes of deities, the
artificer has hung a single glittering jewel
in each eye of the net, and since the net
itself is infinite in dimension, the jewels are
infinite in number"*

Avatamsaka Sutra

I may be digressing from the official Buddhist interpretation
here, but I go on....there exists subtle forms that appear
without the usual factors, such as long-lived beings having
unknown origins, or phenomena, such as space, that are seen
by some to be the support of phenomena. However, they
should not be perceived as ultimate reality or permanent
because they are empty of inherent existence. This includes
God. This would have to include God.

Point eight
Emptiness of the uncomposite:

Chandrakirti states in his famous exposition,

"When arising, cessation and impermanence are not among its characteristics, a phenomenon is known as being uncomposited. They are empty of themselves. This is the emptiness of the uncomposite."

One may continue to abide in the innate view by objecting that if there are no causes and conditions for forms or ideas to arise, it must mean that it is a real support. If the causes and conditions, the primary formula for identifying illusory phenomena, upon penetrating analysis cannot be discovered, then by default this must be something real. No. The truth of the emptiness of the uncomposite, in other words, that which has no causes or conditions, such as the descriptions of God in the bible or other holy religious scriptures, or phenomena such as space, or the tantras is now under scrutiny.

Space is also empty of inherent existence. Simply by existing as open space demonstrates by means of the strict analysis that it also lacks permanence and inherent existence from its own side. Even though many schools of Buddhism see space as being a permanent support of phenomena, here we remove that support as being illusory, if there is a clinging by the innate view. Even what cannot be included in the statement, *"Everything that comes from causes and conditions is empty and illusory,"* is also empty and illusory.

Let us also keep in mind that being uncomposited does not indicate it is conventionally nonexistent. It means that it is empty of the very characteristic we are grasping and clinging toward with our innate view, something that it cannot provide. It cannot be the support of that, and so, even though you might have a strong faith in God and say that God IS, your innate view damages your correct relationship to that process. This is equally true for innate inappropriate grasping of *"I AM"* or any other form of higher relationship with defined uncomposite phenomena. It is upon this misapplication of logic that Buddhists cannot accept a reality relationship with God as permanent.

We are capable of discovering our error by the marvelous logical method of non-affirming negation. We have to take away what it is not, in order to discover what it is and repeat that step until the mind moves into dissolution, the state without foundation. Because that is correct investigation, it is what the analysis induces by the reproducible effect of the Buddhist dharma path to enlightenment.

Returning from that extraordinary experience, the meditator is usually quite convinced that the definitive state has been penetrated, even if that is still not the correct view, because it is a further balanced state of mind. We call that a transitional correct view however, because there are still more layers to be reversed.

Now, let us not be distressed by the aspect of innate view that might be causing us to be unskillful in how we regard God and that relationship. This very point in the analysis, in my opinion, addresses the unskillful, damaged view that forces us, in the name of the respect we direct toward that relationship, to see God as being an ultimate support of our belief in illusory phenomena that binds us to uncontrolled rebirth.

Long lived gods

Subtle forms that appear without the usual factors, such as long-lived beings that have unknown origins to ordinary beings or phenomena that are seen by some, not all, but some, to be the support of phenomena, are not to be worshipped as real and permanent. These do not fall under this point as they are more easily shown to possess causes and conditions upon more careful penetration of higher functioning logical mind. There are also a number of categories of living beings that seem to be all-powerful such as the Greek and Roman gods that are also not to be relied upon as ultimate sources of reality.

The mature believer in a transitional stage of the solidification of belief in permanence perceives that God is not something that can be identified as having come from this cause and that condition, and that God simply IS. According to the analysis, that understanding of God, *"that God is"*, means that its state of arising, cessation, and impermanence in another way of being does not automatically bestow it with reality simply because it is uncomposited and beyond dismantling.

God will not be angry

The belief that is challenged here is not that *"God is not,"* but the inner programming that causes the suffering obstacle of craving permanence. That defective underlying belief should be addressed. It will never be healed if we affirm that everything else, forms, feelings, perceptions, worlds and so forth, are illusory, but continue to rest in a illusory relationship by craving to grasp onto God, Allah, Brahma, or Yahweh as self existing and causeless from its own side, therefore ultimately real. The conceptualization of a being of unknown origin that simple IS, alive without causes or conditions, should mature beyond the unexamined defective relationship that you might presently have with deity.

I have sensed fear of reprisal from their god by believers of one permanent thing to be worshiped, who are capable and ready to skillfully dissolve the innate view that takes the transitory to be permanent. The purpose here is not to damage a careful illusory relationship with God. We will be better Buddhists, Christians or Muslims without the clinging and grasping toward the permanence we desire just as the highest saints of all religions overcame their own fear of being disloyal to God if they entered into a different relationship with deity.

Regarding the method used in Vajrayana Buddhism that incorporates analysis into the practice, HH the Dalai Lama says, *"The emphasis is not on the union of calm abiding and special insight, (which belongs to the non tantric methods of inducing a state of emptiness in the conceptual mind) but on a union of appearance and emptiness qualified by the vivid appearance of one's own mind in the form of a deity and the conceptual realization of emptiness – simultaneously. This is a distinctive assertion of tantra: namely, that an empty phenomenon can appear to a consciousness that is realizing its emptiness conceptually"*

God is not the excellent support for an innate view craving for stability and that is why some people gain insight and later fall away from religious practice and require regular reconverting to a religious doctrine of permanentism. That is a transitional energetic clinging to a virtuous object and at this point in the analysis of the nature of reality, we should no longer be seeing God through the filter of the defective programming of a human realm innate view. God or other uncomposited phenomena are not the excellent support that we are confused into thinking they are. It does not mean that they do not exist or that they do not act as another kind of support, but just not in the way we think they do.

Point nine
Emptiness of that which is beyond extremes:

"That to which extremes do not apply is expressed as being beyond extremes. Its emptiness of its very self is explained as the emptiness of that which is beyond extremes"
Chandrakirti

Chandrakirti here states what is identified as that which is beyond extremes because it actually delineates the various problems that exist on the way to enlightenment. Since the extensive dharma also contains the tools of "not this and not that," here dharma means the characteristic called definitive because it expresses the position regarding absolute truth and is acknowledged to be beyond the extremes of permanentism and nihilism.

Therefore, we do not give up the remedy because it describes the remedy, thinking that True Paths, or higher functioning Dharma might be the first place that you would reject because it is describing cessation.

Some might think that we should reject true paths in order to be alive to the spirit of true paths. I know that sounds convoluted but the mind is tricky and can easily do this.

Many arrive at this stage of intellectual understanding and remain in a view thinking, '*I know now that I do not need to learn anything more. Just knowing that, I have carefully rejected true paths. In honor of its teachings, I reject it.*' This is bizarre, and yet carefully thought out and done by many. They then stop practicing because they think that they now understand it clearly and definitively. Some intelligent Western people have done this but we never do like this in Tibet or we get a smack on the head from our teachers.

It is much better to hold space for the correct dynamic with the path of transformation to emerge at the correct time. We might feel like rushing ourselves and even enjoy a feeling of solidifying around an exciting concept but the skillful practitioner should not act upon it yet. Maintain a steady course in practice, based in reliance, and affirm, "*I am sure I will understand soon.*"

For those who intellectually perceive the philosophical realities of True Paths, it is difficult to see beyond the correct reasoning to the lack of inherent existence or essence. Therefore, we must not give up True Paths in order to find its empty nature, but hold space for that correct relationship with the path of preparation to transformation to emerge at the correct time.

Two views: existence or non-existence

We can look at two extreme philosophical views. Defining and refuting these two views are the foundation and special feature of Buddhism and the middle way philosophy. The philosophy of those who intellectually believe and energetically crave experiencing that there is at least one thing which is permanent are adherents of permanentism, and those who believe that not even one thing can exist are believers in nihilism. That nothing exists, or that at least one true thing exists are the two extremes.

Adherents of most of the world religions believe in permanentism, that at least one thing does exist, such as God. That defines the structured and cultivated illusory outer view but it is the innate view analyzed here where another deeper view is attached to inner minds. That is where the actual programming of human realm that takes the temporary to be permanent is located.

Regarding the other extreme view that nothing exists makes me want to laugh because actually there is not such a thing as a true nihilist. If they were, they would not be here. There would be no way the inner and outer view including the innate view could remain for the second moment after that realization.

The defining characteristic of the Middle Way philosophy is the position of that which is not held by the extremes, and that does not mean that you do a little bit of permanentism and a little bit of nihilism and see how it works together that way, no. So, the two faulty views are similar because they are both extreme without support of either intrinsic reality or logical coherence. What is left after being refuted intellectually and energetically, meaning outer and inner refutation, that remainder is also empty of inherent existence and not the excellent support for your intellectual craving for sensations of knowing.

Point ten
Emptiness of that which has neither beginning nor end:

"That which has no point from which it begins nor boundary where it ends is the cycle of existence. Since it is free from coming and going, it is just mere appearance like a dream. Existence is void of any existence. This is the emptiness of that which neither begins nor ends. It was definitively taught in the commentaries." Chandrakirti

Cyclic existence, the karmic creation and exhaustion of actions over many lives, self replicates and gives rise to a sense of stability and safety that it does not possess. The recycling of samsara gives an unreliable sensation of familiarity that lulls ordinary beings into compliance with an ever-evolving samsaric structure. This circling is all illusory appearance that does not fulfill the promise it seems to make as the excellent support of higher training toward samsaric perfection. The sense of familiarity and learning through experience gives rise to a sense of progress that is by nature without essence.

This means the hope we place and glory we expect to receive within the fascinating evolutionary development contained in samsara that will bring the fulfillment of some imaginary samsaric promise that it seems to make is completely without foundation in samsara, along with the expectation that it will bring the fulfillment of some imaginary samsaric promise it seems to make are all completely without foundation. This includes a sense that everything will be okay in the future or that things are getting better all of the time. The sense of optimism that many people hold gives rise to a feeling of steadiness and protection that samsara does not possess.

Cyclic existence, the succession of births and moving through lives of form, having different kinds of existences does give us a certain sense of personal expertise from a familiarity and security that it does not actually have. However, from a higher view of the path to transformation, it is not good to induce a feeling that existence is dangerous, although in classic Tibetan Buddhism this technique is used to instill a fear of cyclic existence.

Since beginningless time you have wandered in cyclic existence without achieving more than a continuation of cyclic process. The larger dynamic that compels living beings to participate without choices is dreamlike in appearance and empty of inherent reality. Existence itself, as a larger dynamic, is without inherent basis.

Dignity in the rain

So, within the parameters of the existential dilemma that faces all living beings, I end this chapter with a story. Recently I went to our local home improvement center, and when I came out, I had been there so long that I could not remember where I parked my car, and the weather had changed dramatically. It was pouring rain and I had a full shopping cart. The normal reaction would be to run hither and thither in the parking lot, dodging raindrops, trying to find the car. I think you get the picture. However, I decided that, out of a sense of dignity, I was not going to run, as I was not going to get any wetter if I simply walked without scrambling and looking foolish to myself.

In that way, we need not hide or rush from samsara for fear

that we are going to get wet with cyclic existence because we are already, as they say, all wet. With a sense of dignity and an understanding of the true nature of reality, fully prepared beings should be expected to exit cyclic existence with a certain sense of dignity and not like people rushing like mad in the rain.

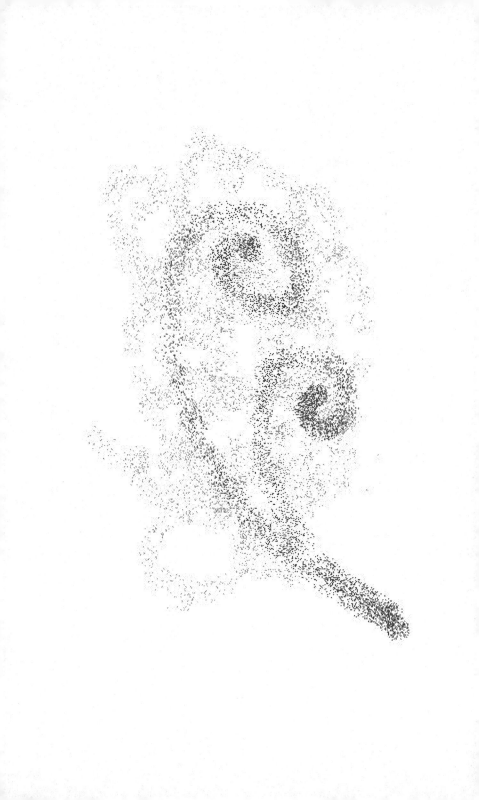

Chapter 11
Reality and Your Religious Bell

"The one thing to be attained is essentially void and compassionate. Let me explain. The realization of voidness is the absolute spirit of enlightenment; it is seeing that all things are unborn. Compassion is the relative spirit of enlightenment; it is reaching out in love to all beings who have yet to realize that they are unborn. Those who follow the Mahayana path should develop these two forms of the spirit of enlightenment."

Drom Tonpa (c.1005-1064)

There are virtuous objects connected to preparation practices for transformation such as Buddha statues, holy texts, and one's lama guiding our progress. Other phenomena not to be discarded are bodhichitta motivation, our meditation practice, and taking responsibility for what we have promised and are able to accomplish in virtue such as dharma service.

Point eleven
Emptiness of what should not be discarded:

"What should not be discarded is empty of itself since this emptiness is its very nature. It is spoken of as the emptiness of what should not be discarded."

Chandrakirti

During cogitation on the analysis or later while meditating, the practitioner is expected to enter into the state without foundation, the perceptual dissolution, which brings them closer to how things actually exist in their own nature. The fact that they do persist in the conventional sense continues to act as a support for gradual transitional understandings. Ordinary reality also continues to support innate confusion, and that confusion as to how they exist should be removed without damaging beneficial uses of the innate view remaining. The meditator will then be capable of learning and practicing further because it is not the purpose to remain in that state without foundation.

Did anybody think that enlightenment is a state with no foundation? One arises in the enlightened state! I think even normal philosophical inquiry sometimes produces different sensations in the body, mind, and energetic system when new logic undermines current understandings.

Bodhichitta and the mentor

The aforementioned, and other objects that aid your practice should be regarded as treasures connected to virtuous karma and are not to be discarded out of a sense that because they are holy and connected to the path to reality, they should be abandoned out of an intellectual understanding of the empty nature of outer and inner objects. Objects such as your mentor and mental constructs, such as bodhichitta, are victoriously empty of inherent existence. Most of them glow with inner aliveness and encouragement toward the correct view.

Even when an immature practice tries to solidify them, these forms persist in being correct objects of virtue toward the transformed state. These precious objects held in esteem do not enter a grinding up of phenomena to decay them so that you can possess their lack of inherent existence from their own side. They are producing a kind of effect toward the correct view because they are already correct objects of virtue. This also applies to bodhichitta motivation and other states of mind helping you toward the transformed state. However, they are also empty of the very thing that holds you away from understanding their true nature as empty of inherent existence.

They are uncontaminated because consecration by means of emptiness holds them in a blessing form as their function. This is why in monasteries everything is reconsecrated regularly. They do rabnye consecration for the images in the temple to repair the blessing because as time goes on, peoples' innate view energetically decays the victorious calling of emptiness.

This is also why holy sites require enlightened beings to visit or to add to the cleansing and refreshing of holy places. Rinpoches are supposed to know how to do this from their training. They are expected to be doing this kind of meditation work whenever they visit sacred places and are encouraged to do that for the benefit of living beings coming to holy places.

Precious objects that have been plunged into emptiness to be cleaned and then blessed are held in esteem and do not enter a kind of grinding up or destruction of all phenomena. They are easily perceived as empty. You might consider destroying all inner traces of phenomena by mentally chewing them up and spitting them out. Do they exist or do they not exist? In order to arrive at the knowledge of their lack of inherent existence, you do not need to do this because they are objects attached to your process of transformation and display their emptiness to help you.

Point twelve
Emptiness of the true nature:

"The true essence of composite and all other phenomena is pure being. Therefore, neither the students, the solitary realizers, the bodhisattvas, nor the Buddhas, created his essence anew. Therefore, this essence of the composite and so forth is said to be the very nature of phenomena. It itself is empty of itself. This is the emptiness of the true nature."

Chandrakirti

Dependent arising is a rational feature of Madhyamika Buddhist philosophy and is a logically coherent understanding of how the world and its contents arise. Understanding this, we must agree that all created phenomena arise due to causes and conditions, whether they are virtuous or nonvirtuous in our estimation.

The descriptions of dependent origination explain how the world and its contents arise not by their own accord, but in dependence on other phenomena. They have no self-power to arise without being a compilation of accompanying factors. Whether a body, a seed, a universe, or a state of mind, dependent origination is a reasonable and easy to understand method of describing our world and ourselves. The application of intellectual understanding of dependent arising is not only coherent in gross manifestation, but it is also consonant with how things exist in higher stages and other realms of existence.

At no time does the Madhyamika Prasangika philosophy depart from the microcosmic or macrocosmic ramifications of Chandrakirti's statement. Not only is this essence, the core of deep wisdom, coherent, it is also consonant. What I mean is, not only does it make logical sense from the ordinary point of view, but it also has a kind of harmonic activity in its correct dynamic more hidden to the probing intellectual mind.

It is consonant with how things exist in higher stages of development and other realms of existence that display higher functioning transitional reality instead of suffering and dysfunctional fantasies. In general, it is good that there is still a blessed connection between what is beyond words and the striving logic of ordinary dwellers of the human realm. This is the bond established by perfection's care between reality beyond the barrier of the innate view and human beings interpreting the Madhyamika philosophy so they can become capable of entering valid relationships with higher-level beings such as buddhas.

Chandrakirti and others invite to the alive state skillfully so that the emerging meditator can come into alignment with correct human valuation of Buddhist learning, thereby entering into emptiness and then into union with the buddha awakened ones via the human realm.

In contrast, the actual way that ordinary, contaminated phenomena exist in generalized form is flaccid and unsatisfactory, but we, in our grasping, are still trying to apply a view of it to cause it to be real. Its actual nature remains beyond the grasp of the innate view that takes the flaccid, transitory, unstable, and temporary to be ultimately real. The path of dharma to the perfected state is clean and pure and will not be subjugated to the inferior view that we grasp toward, so it remains empty.

Reality and early science systems

One of the main obstacles to understanding reality is that the capacity for energetic grasping is attached to your innate view, binding you to a compulsion to see it as real. It is an obstacle procedure when the meditator attempts to subjugate the analysis of ascertaining reality to his or her present understanding of the innate view in the form of a demand for reality to be understood, filtered through an innate view that they are not willing or capable of releasing.

There is no transitional view to the emptiness of true nature. I cannot present a semi-truth other than the words that I use and what you are experiencing while reading these words that explains the nature of what you have not yet understood energetically. This also includes the movement of your mind as well as thinking about how you feel about the experience *"Well, I would like, and then it must…no, it is not that, and then oh… well I cannot…."*

The activity of perceptions stimulates mental and energetic structures which act as a temporary and transitional view toward understanding the nature of all phenomena, but the defining factor for the correct view is that either you have it or you do not have it. There is no semi-correct view. You do not almost have the correct view.

Once we pursue serious study of the emptiness of true nature, the nature of reality continues to remain beyond the grasp of the innate view during the entire study. You are either going to get it, or not. However, the benefit of study and meditation is that now you know that there is something called the correct view that exists beyond the confusion.

Students might correctly question here whether understandings that are transitional views toward correct knowing are okay to stabilize or bring into balance energetically. The answer is yes, so that your energetic being on various levels has time to become familiar and come into alignment with that understanding before awareness moves again into further states of alignment toward the benchmark transformational event of enlightenment.

For example, if given the task of moving a mountain, we would not try to move it by getting a tractor to drag the mountain, but in fact, we might even use some creativity and decide to take the mountain apart bit by bit. That is what I might do. Perhaps then we would take the parts and reassemble it all in another location. However, if we really had to move the whole mountain at once, I would get a very, very big tractor and move it very, very slowly. I might also let the mountain rest in between movements, and that is like transitional stabilization of energies to new ways of being.

Point thirteen
Emptiness of all phenomena:

"The eighteen potentials, the six types of contact, and from those six, the six types of feelings; furthermore, all

that is form and all that is not, the composite and the
uncomposite, this comprises all phenomena".

Chandrakirti

Early materialistic Hindu philosophy, finding the atomist view untenable, moved toward a more interior view of manifestation by developing a system to describe the physical world and its interaction with an inner subtle manifestation of the object.

Briefly, the eighteen elements include twelve sense bases. The eighteen elements are six triads of elements with each triad composed of a sense object, the external sense bases or sense organs, and the internal sense bases which are the associated sense organ consciousness moving and changing the dynamic relationships. In other words, the eighteen elements are made of the twelve sense bases and the six related sense consciousnesses that describe all possibilities of manifestation.

The eighteen potentials, the six types of contact, all that is form and all that is not form, the composite and uncomposite, not only describes, but also comprises all phenomena. It is a useful method of seeing all things as comprised of the eighteen elements in a fluid dynamic relationship with the various sense bases and the six contacts and is still used in Oriental metaphysics. However, from a view that seeks ultimate reality, the Buddha, Nagarjuna, Chandrakirti, and others have refuted these as descriptions of reality and state them to be empty and not the excellent basis for grasping. Although these systems are complex and give a supramundane view to substitute for the less sophisticated matter based atomic-view that they replaced, we should not take them as describing true reality, but as a description of a system of understanding and organizing phenomena.

A system developed and still used in Buddhism is twelve links of interdependent origination, a method describing causes and conditions beyond human life span to illustrate the coming into being, growth, changes, and decay of a living being. The description of the physical world is used in the system only as it relates to the chain of becoming that is a description of suffering, with the main points reflecting a self perpetuating cyclic environment. Beyond these Oriental science systems are the logical tools of the analytical point of view presented by Chandrakirti to gain understanding of reality. This is a different class of early scientific tools, more sophisticated than contemporary science because it includes the refutation of inner perceptions as well as refuting its basis, the outer world. Modern science seduces us into seeking stability by ascribing reality to some materialist scientific development coming in the future.

A way to describe a cup

Concerning point thirteen of the analysis, someone might argue, *"Okay, so phenomena in the form that they are appearing to me, such as a post or a cup, let us just say that I agree with you, Rinpoche, that this is empty, just for argument's sake. However, in fact there have been philosophers that have very carefully thought about these things and have stated that, of course the world is not what it appears to be! I have studied, I am an adept in understanding the nature of reality based upon how it actually appears as an interaction of the eighteen elements in relation to the inner bases, so my system is correct to say that phenomena do not appear in the way that we think they do. They appear as objects and results of the eighteen elements. Reality is described as a combination of the eighteen elements."*

This would not actually refute point thirteen, as Chandrakirti here is only opening the discussion that will be addressed in point fourteen. Here we already have controversies whether the system is defining phenomena or going beyond that permission and leading others to rely on it as a reality description. These systems are material or immaterial quantifiers. I might find it useful to know how long my nose is, but does that help me to know my true nature?

Many people who desire to know truth believe that if they only had time to enter into a course of study such as the eighteen potentials, astrology or the chakra system, they would be able to understand the nature of reality. This may lead to uneducated faith toward what will not satisfy. For those who actually do enter and study, the adherents of various systems become quite convinced that their system is the superior one for discovering reality when it is only science describing phenomena and remains unenlightened and unconnected to true source.

That is what their scholars say: *"If I could take an hour or two of your time, Rinpoche, to discuss my system you could understand the eighteen potentials. I am sure that you would then have a better grasp on the nature of reality because the eighteen potentials is the only system that will explain that."* Many people in spiritual development today believe there is also a connection between the nature of reality and truth of the chakras and there is not! This system was created as a method for purification, and it is actually part of Buddhist training. Nevertheless, Buddhist or not, I still affirm it is only a system and not the excellent basis for grasping.

However, regarding the chakras, when receiving training by some, you are given to believe that the chakras actually exist in some true reality form in a way that is consonant with their system, when in fact they do not. It is better to view them as tools and not worship the system as being the excellent support for the grasping of your innate view.

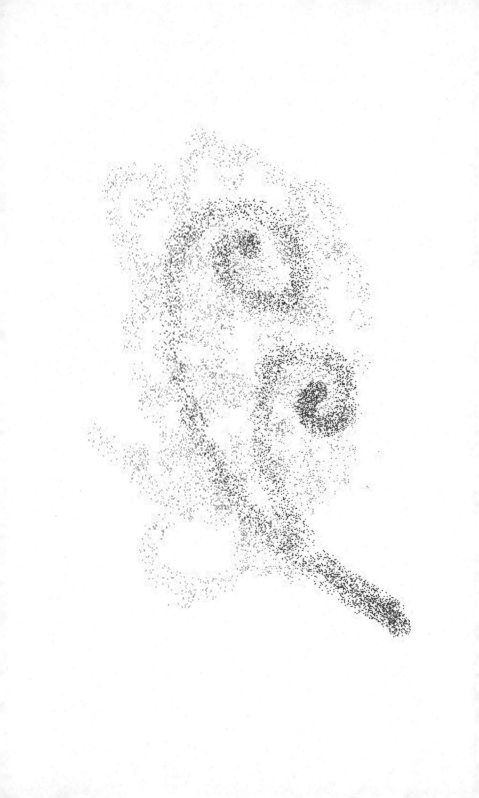

Chapter 12
Reality and Keeping Ducks in a Row

The greatest achievement is selflessness.
The greatest worth is self-mastery.
The greatest quality is seeking to serve others.
The greatest precept is continual awareness.
The greatest medicine is the emptiness of everything.
The greatest action is not conforming with the world's ways.

The greatest magic is transmuting the passions.
The greatest generosity is non-attachment.
The greatest goodness is a peaceful mind.
The greatest patience is humility.
The greatest effort is not concerned with results.
The greatest meditation is a mind that lets go.
The greatest wisdom is seeing through appearances.

Atisha

Even though systems such as science, eighteen dharmas, sacred geometry, chakras, and more describe in detail the minute distinctions between abstruse points while defining phenomena, the results of that specialized study and scientific inquiry will not cause what is transitory to be intrinsically real. There are implied affirmations that these methods are wisdom truth devices that reveal the knowledge of true reality. Even sophisticated techniques considered secret or esoteric are empty of existence from their own side and are products of conceptual manifestation depending upon other elements, causes, and conditions.

Point fourteen
Emptiness of defining characteristics:

Great Sage Chandrakirti states in his analysis to ascertain reality, "*All composite and uncomposite phenomena have their own individual defining characteristics. These are empty of being themselves. This is the emptiness of defining characteristics.*"

The discriminations we consign to what is real and what is unreal still depend on our point of view, deciding what is either materialistic or of a spiritual nature while we are still within the grasp of the innate view. This view that takes the transitory and illusory to be real cannot even hold the more advanced view of the composite and uncomposite simultaneously without mixing the characteristics that make them unique in manifestation.

This attempt to synthesize a new view of compounded phenomena by making it like an uncompounded manifestation creates confusion that solidifies into attitudes such as thinking that reality arises into forms by unusual methods while the person is still under the influence of, and relying on, the innate view.

Nirvana and space

Nirvana, or cessation, and space are considered examples of uncompounded phenomena and are also empty of inherent existence even though they are not considered to have parts. Composite and uncomposite phenomena have a common valuation in their lack of true reality, but still remain valid in manifestation for the one holding the correct conventional view. Rather than the removal of all irritations and elements of suffering, it is important to realize that true correct view sees the emptiness of phenomena without disrespecting it.

Do not damage phenomena

The skillful use of analysis requires us to make subtle separations of data into different categories without damaging the data. For example, a delicate flower we wish to understand needs to be in an environment that supports its continuation such as a garden or a vase of water as we observe it. In a similar manner, the mind is delicate and sophisticated in its many functions. Some of these functions are transmuting, while others will remain coherent with an emerging worldview that causes the meditator to be able to be of benefit to others by having a competent mind.

Therefore, the prepared analyst of emptiness will relax a bit in body and mind so that they receive the true benefit of understanding that appearances continue to manifest with functional characteristics while simultaneously displaying their common nature of lack of intrinsic existence.

Point fifteen
Emptiness of the imperceptible:

"The present does not remain. The past and future do not exist; wherever you look, you cannot see them, so the three times are called imperceptible. The imperceptible is in essence empty of itself. It is neither permanent and stable nor impermanent and fleeting. This is the emptiness of the imperceptible."

Chandrakirti

Chandrakirti states from a logical philosophical position that even the smallest duration of time cannot hold what is illusory. Therefore, not even the smallest moment of time has the natural structural capacity to hold what is truly real. Because it has no inherent reality, it is empty of inherent self-sustaining existence, and because of that, its appearance is illusory.

Looking for the present moment presents a difficulty, as there seems to be no division of time small enough to hold it! When we observe even more carefully, past and future press upon and seem to consume the present. However, if we shift our approach, it is possible to perceive a flowing current of unimpeded Nows that exist in and through us and through all of creation. The balanced feeling that arises in the energetic human body is extraordinarily pleasant and heals all anxiety and stress. This comfortable dynamic is meant to be the normal method of ordinary humans interacting with others and their environment. Actions can be performed effortlessly. This is also a more skillful relationship with the human innate view.

The flow of pleasant NOW

Even then, by mistaking what is changeable and impermanent to be a permanent state, the adherent of the flow of pleasant Now can solidify and grasp toward happiness or crave the pleasant feeling and, in that way, miss the transformation needed for evolutionary development. Because it is still based in the defective view, this precarious position can be easily shaken by events, and one can become angry and disappointed because their peace was disturbed, blaming and struggling to regain what now only exists in the past as a memory of peace. However, once the innate view is eroded and eventually dismantled, the easy flow of Now becomes natural because one perceives the lack of intrinsic reality of the present moment.

Time

As for the analysis, the past, by definition, is gone, and the future, by definition, has not yet arrived, and the present slips by so fast that by the time you have found this now, it is past! This traditional inquiry is done in order to deflate our false sense of security that causes us to believe that time is the excellent support for the craving mind to perform its restless activities. Without grasping toward time, all the structures that depend on time collapse carefully.

Further, for the less mature, I suggest that the preliminary inquiry into time include an intellectual understanding and cogitation meditations on the unsteady and transitory nature of time by its own appearances as a conceptual construct of the perceptions. That means our perception of time is unreasonably flexible. We anthropomorphize time by fantasizing that time bestows happiness to enjoy life, but ends it too soon, while time causes our suffering to go on and on endlessly without hope that time itself will release its grasp on us so our suffering will end

Holding away change

A solidification of perception of time gives unnecessary strength to the innate view that creates the baseline suffering of attempting to hold back change or momentary change. Even within states of happiness, our grasping and clinging to events combined with conceptual time tries to prevent change, and that suffering is real to the innate view holder.

All the possible relationships with linear, event-based, life process are only convenient fictions to mark the passage that begins with birth and ends in death to a person living in the human realm.

It is possible to discover and refute time as an unsupported perceptual construct. This is accomplished by making only a small amount of investigative effort to understand that time does not have structure itself, but only perceived illusory effects and is easily penetrated by ordinary scrutiny. The deeper valuations of time based on momentary change can only be perceived in deep meditation and that will remain unanalyzed until then. This very deep and innate structure is what Chandrakirti views as imperceptible time. However, ordinary perceptual time is identified as possessing an evanescent and imperceptible quality, and that does not imbue it with a sacred transcendent reality. Quite the opposite, it is a fancy frill of civilizations decline.

Point sixteen
Emptiness that is the absence of entities:

"Since an entity arises from causes and conditions, it lacks the nature of being a composite. This emptiness of there being anything that is a composite is the emptiness that is the absence of entities."

Chandrakirti

Since we need to gradually become familiar with the intellectually held correct view, the discussion of lack of reality of the self is last in the analysis so that we do not develop fear but have a good grounding and success in the dismantling of our innate view. Entity is self, the unseen overarching, organizing principle that uses ego, mind, and perceptions to maintain an intact illusion of the innate view.

Self does not arise without a function

Self is a subtle object that arises due to causes and conditions and transcends the gathering of elements by having a function of bestowing names to what is other than itself. The self performs this activity based on the appearance of, and in dependence on, causes and conditions and does not arise without a function. The self as a perceptual construct, is not comprised of parts, as its function is not related to either the completed assembly or to the individual nature of parts that comprise a person.

Self does not exist without a function

However, the self cannot exist without its functions. Because of that, upon analysis, the ordinary self that provides a structure for the innate view can be dissolved and the person can assume a conventional identity without the innate view. The self's function is bare perception. Without performing a naming function, the inappropriate self would be part of an assembly that had taken the whole to be its possession. In the former case, the self would be a correct view of a manifested composite object

We cannot prevent naming

So, if you try consciously as much as you can to avoid naming the result of causes and conditions in order for it to have a special status in reality, it will still not make it ultimately real. In other words, if you mentally struggle to prevent the result of causes and conditions coming to your mind, in order to perceive its reality, this will not help. The relationship you have with objects and others is not based in reality. You cannot see things as careful conventional composites or whole things that simply exist from causes and conditions. Instead, you grasp the filter of the innate view that solidifies this bare perception function into an ordinary self that names phenomena in order to perceive them.

A new kind of self

We need to facilitate a correct destruction of the ordinary self and its lower functions while still retaining the naming function in a transmuted self. This new identity comes alive in a more subtle form because of skillful preparation in bodhichitta compassion practices. This new transitional "self" is still emanated but now the actual being has moved into a more subtle form that is capable of perceiving both the empty nature and conventional reality.

Without an inner quantum shift in perception that does not contain the innate view programming, the benefits of a correct conventional view after enlightenment, including the imbuing of perceptual orientation, would result in mental confusion. To attempt to stabilize enlightenment without good grounding in what to expect in the expanded correct view would not be so useful.

The stabilizing of transitional views causes us to have different attitudes and relationships toward ourselves and the "self". Whether we have the view that holds the self to be real, or to be non-existent, or to be an evolving product of evolutionary development toward perfection, the object of our search, once found, is also empty of inherent existence.

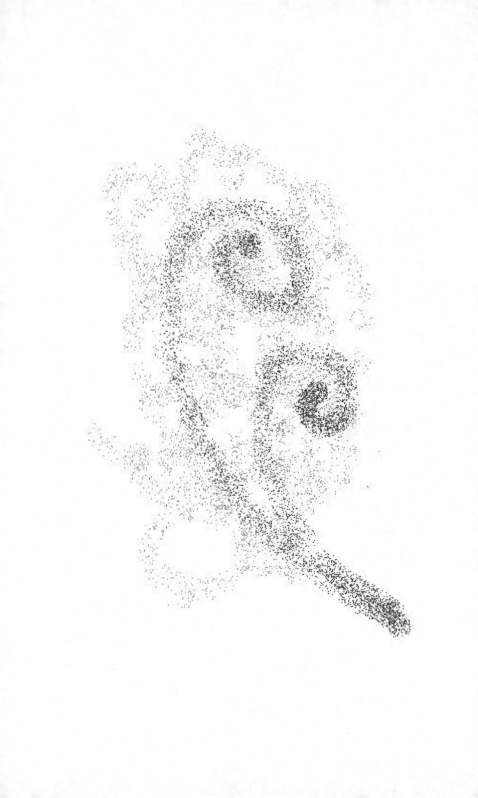

Chapter 13
Summary of Sixteen Emptinesses
Makes Twenty

"As your insight into the ultimate nature of reality is deepened and enhanced, you will develop a perception of reality from which you will perceive phenomena and events as sort of illusory, illusion-like, and this mode of perceiving reality will permeate all your interactions with reality. Even emptiness itself, which is seen as the ultimate nature of reality, is not absolute, nor does it exist independently. We cannot conceive of emptiness as independent of a basis of phenomena, because when we examine the nature of reality, we find that it is empty of inherent existence. Then if we are to take that emptiness itself is an object and look for its essence, again we will find that it is empty of inherent existence. Therefore the Buddha taught the emptiness of emptiness."

The Art of Living the 14th Dalai Lama

The Sixteen Emptinesses are now condensed into four classes of emptinesses serving as a summary of the previous sixteen and are the elements of a tetralemma logical statement of Nagarjuna. His work, hundreds of years before Chandrakirti, would have probably been lost without Chandrakirti's elucidation. They are called Holy Father and Son in early Indian Buddhism and are the founders of the Middle Way view which defines the highest Buddhist views of reality. Nagarjuna's summary states:

*"It is not realism. It is not nihilism. It is not dualism, and
it is not monism. It is not permanent. It is not, not there.
It is not two, and it is not one. This is the emptiness of the
four extreme positions."*

Point one
Emptiness of entities:

*"That which is named. In other words, not permanentism
Everything included in the five aggregates."*

Chandrakirti

The first point rejects the relative world of apparent reality
as not possessing the marks and signs of ultimate reality.
This aphorism states the position refuting or denying
permanentism or realism. Emptiness of everything means
that what is perceived inside as feelings and thoughts,
outside as sense objects other than "me," as well as the
object we call "I and me", do not arise by their own power,
but solely depend on other causes to arise. This is true
whether it is accomplished by karmic means, stimulation
of the environment, interacting with others, stimulating our
own mind, or even by the interaction of perceptions, creating
further ideas or concepts. We cannot say that everything out
there is nonexistent and only I exist. Neither can we assert
the opposite, both positions, or neither. The interdependent
nature of manifested existence acknowledges the lack of
ultimate base of reality.

What is perceived by inner and outer senses as well as the
products of those perceptions, as well as the products of the
products of thinking are all illusory. For example, I think

I should move a chair to a different place so I send Joe out to move it, and when he moves the chair a bee stings him. All activities instigated by inner and outer minds, as well as the products of that activity, such as somebody else being stung by a bee also logically lack reality no matter how far from the original idea the actions take place. The gathering of concepts expanded by Chandrakirti and commentary can now be synthesized after being clearly understood in detailed form. This also encourages the analyst meditator to now develop a feeling tone of the analysis while still retaining the understanding. This allows the correct intellectual view to move away from merely words to higher functioning intelligence tending toward the correct view.

Point two
Emptiness of nonentities:

> *In short, "non-entities" are*
> *All un-composite phenomena.*
> *Non-entities are empty of being non-entities,*
> *And this is the "emptiness of non-entities."*
>
> Chandrakirti

Cessation is by nature without causes or conditions and non-existent. When the delusions that require an innate view as a support are destroyed by the wisdom of reality, they cease to exist in the special manner as functions of a disfigured dynamic. Since they existed in the past due to the afflictions of craving and grasping of ordinary mind, there does remain a memory, *"This was a suffering state that I have left, and now I am free."* This special cessation is also induced by the very process that created the correct trajectory to arrive at the place of developing wisdom in the individual. This means that even when everything is done correctly and one arrives at the correct view, even this cessation is illusory, dream-like, and empty. This is very nice, isn't it?

The third noncomposite phenomena are a class of strange data called ordinary cessation. For example, there is no ox, no elephant, and no snake in this room. Fantasy figments of imagination that are not possible to exist such as the horns of a rabbit or the child of a barren woman, in philosophical argument, are of this category. They are not only nonexistent in ordinary terms but also empty of inherent existence in their supposed existence. In that way, we cannot take refuge in fantasy objects or recreate enlightened beings as a kind of fantasy deity as an alternative to seeing things as they are. Believers in permanentism can fall into this error in their attempt to not listen to the ordinary world and create a fantasy world of their own making, to rest and feed their craving mind.

Point three
Emptiness of the nature:

"The nature of phenomena is that they have no essence.
It is called their nature because no one created it.
The nature is empty of itself, and this is the emptiness
of the nature."

Chandrakirti

After all signs of manifestation of phenomena are removed and caused to dissolve as unsupported by logical analysis, there still remains an elusive quality to the residue. This deep object of subtle clinging is also without essence. However much we wish to avoid naming it, the innate view programming that holds us away from our true nature continues to give it a name that it does not actually possess. We cannot fall into the error of espousing a belief in the nature of how phenomena exist in reality while remaining intact in the innate wrong view. Everything that can be named is empty and without the excellent support we might wish to have for our spiritual pride.

Point four
Emptiness of the entity that is other:

"Whether or not Buddhas appear in the world, the natural emptiness of all entities is proclaimed to be the entity that is other. Other names for this are the genuine limit and suchness. They are empty of themselves, and this is the emptiness of the entity that is other."

Chandrakirti

There is no struggle for objects and phenomena such as inner events, ideas, feelings, as well as sky, clouds, mountains, and other persons, and yourself, to exist in reality. Your struggle is to lose the hypnotic trance that holds you to a way of being in your body, mind, world, and cosmos, which is antithetical to how it actually exists. This distorted view is suffering itself. This intense remainder that is the essence of a noncomposite assembly is also empty of inherent existence.

Part Three

Unfolding
the Mystery
of
Emptiness & Love

Chapter 14
Compassion of the Wisdom Bodhisattva
(Training Practices after Enlightenment)

*"May I be a guide for those who do not have a guide, a
leader for those who journey, a boat for those who cross
over, and all sorts of ships, bridges, beautiful parks for
those who desire them, and light for those who need light.
May I also become the basic conditions for all
sentient beings, such as earth or even the sky, which is
indestructible."*

Shantideva - Bodhicharyavatara

We now turn our attention to the compassion of bodhisattva
wisdom, after having completed Twenty Emptinesses of
Chandrakirti. This important work clarified Nagarjuna's
thinking and answered many questions that arose in early
times regarding Nagarjuna's dramatic new Middle Way
philosophy on the nature of reality. In Tibetan scholarly
study, the writings and teachings of Chandrakirti are equal
in importance to the writings and teachings of Nagarjuna.
Many scholars and practitioners feel that without
Chandrakirti, Nagarjuna's presentation would have been
lost due to the difficulty of understanding what he meant.
For anyone who has ever respectfully opened a book by
Nagarjuna but not comprehended it, Chandrakirti has done
us a great service. In his writings, this enlightened being
was not just parroting or struggling to understand what

Nagarjuna said. Chandrakirti had original thinking and fearlessly opened up new levels of inquiry.

At this point in our emerging relationship, you, the reader, might also have questions regarding Chandrakirti's commentary, or my own. For that reason, I asked myself some of the questions that you might ask, beginning with, "*Rinpoche, if everything is devoid of the very thing that I believe is solid, real, and trustworthy inside and outside... if the past, the present, and the future, and even the bodhisattvas are not the really real entities that I think they are, then how do bodhisattvas generate bodhichitta?*" I asked the question, and then I had to think about it for a while...

Actual bodhichitta is an authentic inner sense. In preparation practices and training, we learn what is possible and what needs to be accomplished while still in the human realm with a human body, human mind, and an innate view. If the preparation practices did not take into account that we have an innate view that sees the changeable as permanent, they would simply be other philosophical musings without practical application, isn't that so?

Preparation practices created for trainees do take the innate view into account. The path and guidance do not require us to be perfect or to hide our lack of perfection while we try to accomplish the important task of transformation toward perfection. If this were the case, then a logical trap would be created: only the perfect could become enlightened! It is our good luck that it does not work that way.

Protected by the innate view

We can look at the innate view in the way a cocoon gives the caterpillar the parameters needed to emerge into another way of being. Like a butterfly yet to emerge, we must make the effort to become released from the protection of the innate view to become strong enough to enter into another phase of development. If that change is made with awareness, the remainder of transformative bodhichitta practices awaits the newly enlightened being beyond the state that required human innate programming.

In order to become prepared to enter another way of being suitable for learning more, the meditator must enter into a special anteroom, devoid of the innate view that perceptually solidifies that which is not intrinsically real. If this change is made carefully, the candidate will be prepared to enter further bodhichitta practices.

Energetic transformation accomplished previously in the human realm will cause us to energetically reject the lower nirvana of liberation for ourselves alone so that we instead move onto other practices and further experiences to become benefit beings. Because some are not capable of that, when thay are presented with the transformative calling, they will enter the cessation of liberation and will be no more.

Alternatively, some may enter into a stasis cessation, but with a need to satisfy some karmic result; they will eventually fall away from karmic temporary cessation, assume form, and perhaps even return to ordinary being. Not everyone is capable of the bodhichitta path. Not everyone has the powerful desire awakening, which says,

"*I want to be of benefit to all living beings.*" That is why bodhichitta motivation is unique; it will be you, not someone else, who will experience the change of mind to become a new benefit being. When that training has not yet been completed, confusion of the actual way we are alive acts like a membrane that holds us away from all of vast life during training. The same confusion also holds us away from all of life while we are trapped in cyclic existence, unable to leave or do as we wish with our life.

After bodhisattvas go through many different kinds of training in numerous perceptual world spheres and purelands, they become so skillful and needed that they are valuable resources to living beings and should continue to benefit many for as long as possible. Eventually, they become so skillful that they become candidates for entering perfection itself, as though they could not help it.

Dharmakaya

What will be described here are qualities and activities of dharmakaya, but I have noticed the word dharmakaya has changed and become more related to interior human activities. The meaning of dharmakaya has become too familiar, so everybody who is anyone is in the "dharmakaya sphere." It has become a term of social dharmic respect and no longer refers to the actual quality of dharmakaya, as it was understood in ancient days by interior enlightened standards.

We need to return to the correct meaning of perfection, beyond this lowered standard that characterizes dharmakaya as a knowable quality and a term to be so casually used. There are many different levels, trainings, purifications, and processes that a living being needs before entering the perfected state. For simplicity of explanation, it is not possible to jump right from understanding lack of inherent existence to the perfected state of dharmakaya.

Great compassion

Even though bodhisattvas will reject the lower Nirvana repeatedly, at a certain point they become candidates for entering the perfected state. This is what we acknowledge to be a Parinirvana, the state from which no further human emanations are performed by the buddha level being. They transcended whatever state of being they were in as they enter complete and total buddhahood. After entering the absolutely perfected state, their nature and the nature of perfection are not different.

Then, from perfection emanates an intention that has the ability to enter into any form through manifestation. However, even when arriving at the gate of human perceptual realm, emanations from perfection have not moved from perfection. Buddha level beings are capable of observing the needs of living beings because they abide in perfection. The fully enlightened ones are not here to satisfy our every need, but to observe and free perfection itself living under poor dynamics in the form of suffering ordinary beings.

The concern that they feel, and their capacity to free obstacles to development, is called Great Compassion. Great Compassion can only be generated from the perfected state. All of the careful training bodhisattvas receive on the way to perfection is based on compassion and now corrected use of inner sense bases. Therefore, they use their transformed inner bases and senses just as you use the human mind, human body, and innate view to correctly generate your own stage of compassion. Why is this so? Compassion is so extremely important; you must *become* compassion.

'... the wisdom of emptiness must be accompanied by a motivation of deep concern for others (and by the compassionate deeds it inspires) before it can remove the obstructions to omniscience, which are the predispositions for the false appearance of phenomena—even to sense consciousness—as if they inherently exist. "

His Holiness the Dalai Lama

Bodhisattvas learn how to use the senses

Let us leave aside how ordinary people see compassion and think a bit about correct training in the human development of compassion and other higher training. There are various training stages that are possible; correct human compassion, followed by compassion training received by bodhisattvas, and finally, training in Great Compassion that comes from the perfected state.

Human beings are capable of learning how to correctly use outer bases or outer/inner bases to clearly understand the correct compassion of a practitioner. The outer sense bases are identified as eye, ear, etc., connected to inner eye and inner ear, and so on up to consciousness/awareness interacting with self, others, and the environment. The activity of these levels interacting restlessly processes energetic data into meaning. Your inner strategy for being alive, whatever level of development you might have, depends upon the meaning created by this process. Incoming data easily becomes polluted by anger, trauma and other dysfunctions that prevent the altruistic motivation of compassion from being active. Our capacity to learn and experience human compassion in preparation for the enlightened state must be healed quickly. Because compassion is vital to transformation, preparation involves many steps and levels to help us become skillful.

After enlightenment, compassion, combined with a cultivated sense of universal responsibility, should remain even though the illusion of the innate view is broken. Here, I make a distinction between what I call learner bodhisattvas and buddha emanated bodhisattvas. The learner bodhisattva uses prepared, but only partially developed, inner sense bases to continue learning correct compassion. This new form of compassion, true bodhichitta, is the enlightened vast source of boundless energy that makes it possible to benefit limitless living beings.

In order to be of most benefit, the bodhisattvas who guide living beings to liberation or enlightenment remain away from human realm dense energies. Since bodhisattvas are beyond the need to stimulate their senses in order to satisfy personal desires that cause stress and confusion, they wisely remain beyond form in the correct manner. They do not often enter into situations where they will need to activate the illusory sense bases of a human being and the innate view that will create illusory and painful karma that they do not actually have. That means very few bodhisattvas emanate into the human realm in comparison to their vast numbers.

The Bodhisattva finally enters perfection

These learner bodhisattvas will ultimately enter perfection

after eons of experience skillfully benefiting others while remaining under the care and guidance of Buddha level beings. After passing through more developed states, they eventually enter buddhahood, a defined state of being, now devoid of all stains that previously prevented the omniscient state from arising.

It is also good for us to understand that the state of buddha is natural in some living beings that never entered ordinary existence, so that we can avoid the error of thinking that all buddhas were once suffering human beings. However, having come from the suffering state and received the transformations, entry by a bodhisattva into buddhahood is a cause for rejoicing in higher-level beings. After this attainment, that Buddha is able to emanate forms at will and becomes skillful in bodhisattva activity by emanation, while the inner base resides in the stillness of perfection. It is uncertain at what skill level a buddha enters perfection completely. However, this entry into perfection stills all inner perceived activities.

Perfection continues to emanate forms such as buddhas from absolute balance and stillness through Great Compassion, compelled by the needs of living beings. The emanation process from perfection, to buddha, to their emanations of myriad bodhisattvas, is a miracle of compassion and highest universal responsibility only possible from that sublime nature. Buddha emanated bodhisattvas do not usually enter the sense organs and the sense bases, but remain in a viable and subtle form. Some of these forms are identified as deities, while the true identity of all buddha emanated bodhisattvas remains in perfection's sphere.

What is a sentient being?

Who are the objects of the care of a great compassion bodhisattva? Perfected in wisdom, buddha emanated bodhisattva's activity is toward sentient beings of different categories. Sentient beings, or living beings, are those who are not yet enlightened or awakened to the illusory nature of ordinary reality. Sentient beings exist in many forms, realms, and locations and even in formless realms. The lost ones, the suffering sentient beings, are not actively being nurtured in development because they are not prepared enough to receive specialized care.

As healing by myriad methods reverses damage to inner levels of suffering beings, gradually all of them will become capable of receiving direct care. In a technical sense, a careful practitioner is in a category of beings that are cared for and nurtured in the development stage and is therefore not a sentient being. However, sometimes a practitioner is a sentient being, and sometimes a practitioner is not a sentient being. The one who is strongly practicing is lifted to higher development temporarily, but easily falls back into samsara. Due to samsara and individual karma, this higher state is not continuous for them, and bursts of practice enthusiasm are often followed by periods of inappropriate suffering. Because of this, practitioners are generally also called suffering sentient beings.

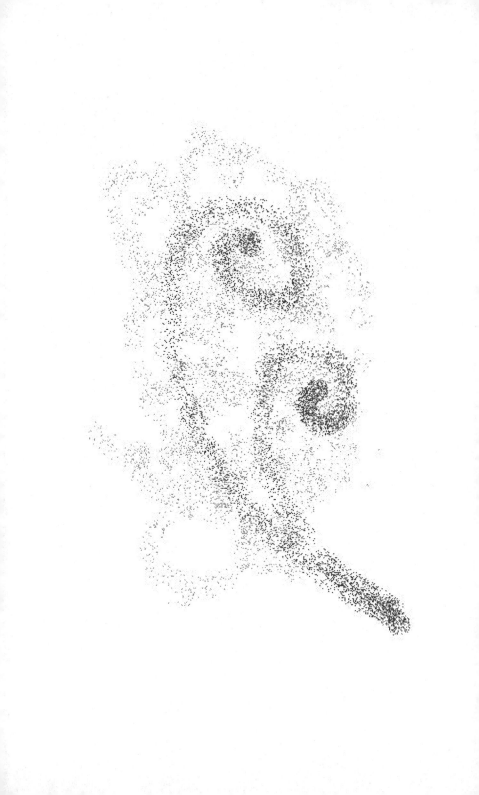

Chapter 15
Compassion of Wisdom toward the Shaky Mind

"Therefore, Sariputra, it is because of his non-attainment that a Bodhisattva, through having relied on the Perfection of Wisdom, dwells without thought-coverings. In the absence of thought-coverings, he has not been made to tremble, he has overcome what can upset, and in the end, he attains to Nirvana"

The Heart Sutra

The next question I ask on your behalf is, *"How do bodhisattvas maintain the equilibrium of seeing things as they are, empty of inherent existence, and still see the point of view of suffering sentient beings?"* The nature of the perfected state is creativity. Otherwise, how could it possibly ever untangle the knots of confusion and help us become free? Bodhisattva activity is supramundane creativity, aligning others with higher being and purifying with joyful energies.

There are different classes of bodhisattvas, and most of these enlightened beings do not approach the sense fields of ordinary beings out of a correct concern of being imprinted by ordinary minds. Their healing work is possible because, holding compassion, they can heal injured energies of the suffering being without taking on characteristics of illusory karma. New bodhisattvas still contain stains of ordinary experience even though the production of dysfunctions ceased after enlightenment, so they must be particularly careful in this way. New practitioners, in preparation to awaken, energize themselves through inquiry into the nature of reality and create really strange ideas about what is and what is not enlightenment. They, too, must be particularly careful of the ramifications of form realms.

A lack of correct perceptions can become prematurely mixed with energies freed before higher alignment is achieved. The grasping mind craves to realign newly released energies into either the original contaminated form or a different contaminated fantasy form.

At this point, some meditators are apt to create or play with an inner deity like a character or a different form than the one indicated by inner bodhisattva guiding toward perfection. Out of a sense of new familiarity with blessing beings, Western people often treat inner mentor or deity like a personal buddy, and become casual at the very time they are being invited to learn correct relationships.

Rare and special alignment

As these energies are released by removing blockages, balancing confused states of mind while the innate view is still being challenged on a more interior level, the natural impulse is to draw these energies back into the familiar but contaminated pattern. Getting up from meditation, the meditator often shakes himself or herself back into the usual dynamic they engaged in before. The rare and special guidance toward perfection is an alignment that perhaps we have not yet experienced, and so we need information to behave appropriately when the opportunity for alignment arrives.

Buddha emanated bodhisattvas are specially trained to avoid entanglement in confused minds. It is dangerous work for extremely subtle beings to adapt to interacting with gross energy beings, such as human beings. The practitioner does preparation practices, takes vows to purify him or herself, and is cautioned repeatedly to remain calm and not be caught up in agitation, fear, blame, or doubt regarding practice or their environment. When the grasping mind is freeing energies that caused suffering for a very long time; the rule is: Do not disturb or annoy your own mind. This is **NOT** a suggestion!

Respecting the mentor and yourself

It is also important not to disturb the mind of our mentor, who is facilitating our understanding of the preparations needed for transformation. The mental models presented in his or her teachings will change the practitioners' thinking enough to make them candidates for inner guidance being who facilitates the process for inner minds. Not only that, but outer mentor, already aligned to buddha guidance being, acts as advocate for our process. In the ordinary sense, we always interact with our outer mentor in ways that do not disrupt their meditation or, for trivial reasons, take them away from inner work they are doing for the benefit of many. When we do contact the lama, we do it calmly and also without disturbing our own mind. This is what real practitioners do.

We have a further responsibility to respect our inner processes and ourselves. Inner mentor, the bodhisattva or buddha level being, needs us to maintain an energetically quiet atmosphere to assist in the transformation of the inner process. When there is quiet inside and outside, the conditions of this world system will be aligned to provide a careful practice environment. The power of the wisdom buddha emanated bodhisattva acts as a midwife for the transformation stage through inner encouragement and cautioning, and by helping the birthing process. Since all living beings are perfection itself, do not know it, and cause suffering for themselves and others by that misknowledge, the wisdom bodhisattva teaches out of compassion.

Self-cherishing and trust

My next question is, *"Rinpoche, if I am not doing preparation and meditation correctly and feel like I am getting caught up in self-cherishing, how do I understand that inner mentor is still with me and performing acts of compassion toward me when I become distorted?"*

For the benefit of all sentient beings who will benefit from our activities in the future, we all want preparation for alignment to go steadily and smoothly even while we are operating within an innate view that seems to encourage confusion. For someone with faith and trust in the Buddha, the dharma practices of transformation, and the sangha of enlightened ones, the inner glance from compassion wisdom bodhisattva instantly relaxes and smoothly aligns our innermost being more closely with enlightened, vast being. This smooth transition results from preparation by meditation and purification.

Making the Bodhisattva into a devil

However, that very same glance for the confused can feel awful and punishing. The cause of this confusion might only be a temporary obstacle that prevents the meditator from gaining the alignment by inner bodhisattva. However, a skillful practitioner will throw away contaminated ideas arising from confusion far away and resume his or her relationship with inner mentor based on love and trust without looking at the confusion.

The unskillful practitioner will make a bodhisattva into a devil and develop poor habits such as an aversion to blessings and constricting their energy instead of relaxing it at the appropriate times. If this is not healed, over time the meditator will become a rough person. To a certain extent, the inhabitants of this world have become rough and incapable of receiving enlightened touch. The Tantric path of Tibetan Buddhism has become specialized in helping people out of this seemingly impossible dilemma.

Without faith and because of unsteadiness in practice, practitioners who flip from trust and faith to mistrust and confusion are difficult to train in the higher tantras. They properly belong to Baby Buddhism and not to higher trainings. If we wish to receive the higher trainings, in addition to faith, we must have some level of control over conflicting emotions. Even from a state of deep energetic confusion regarding the way we actually exist, the meditator still needs to take personal responsibility and learn discipline. Those who are controlled by conflicting emotions are not suitable for higher trainings.

We are not expected to be perfect in order to be a good practitioner. However, we must affirm that there is nothing to be afraid of, and no one is trying to harm us. The roiling up of purification process might cause strange thinking, such as, '*Oh my gosh, I felt a bump,*' or '*Somebody looked at me! I thought I saw something that looked like a dark shape.*' Let us get control over the emotions so we can really be practitioners and not just interested bystanders. Practices such as Chod and other inner trauma healing techniques will begin recovery from a deep basis while the practitioner makes efforts in stabilizing new behaviors. Of course, we do not want to be afraid when wisdom bodhisattva comes and touches us; that would be inappropriate.

This is not Baby Buddhism

My personal lineage in Tibet worked with meditators who were highly trained and even with initiating lamas who received the inner guidance, and midwife-type process of transformation for their own development. Do not force me, or your present qualified lama, to be a Baby Buddhism teacher when you could be capable of higher practices. From the great Bodhisattvas, Buddhas and Perfection itself, you are being called to your true home. There are myriad experiences and trainings you will need before then. The buddhas, who have compassion for your confusion, will touch you and all sentient beings again and again on the interior to see who is ready for transformation in accordance with the deep law. Be ready, and be receptive to that touch.

Personality and ego

Our identities are mixed with our personalities, and we take quite a bit of pride in the upkeep of these constructs.

However, if we look at this situation more objectively using higher motivation, we can view personality as a set of strategies that we have developed to interact with others, our environment, and even ourselves that can be adapted for helping us maintain high standards. Up until now, we have perhaps not really analyzed the origin or ramifications of these strategies. Buddhism teaches us how to have a better relationship with self, others, and the world without exclusively leaning on strategies of old personality habits to accomplish life's important tasks.

Relying on practiced ego-centered interactions with the gross senses is not as healthy or alive as learning and using higher dynamics. Through understanding the illusory nature of ordinary reality, we are freed from exclusive use of rote personality strategies that often become mixed with our dysfunctions. By putting into practice what we learn on the dharmic path, we can see the world freshly and clearly, no longer compelled by our collection of habitual strategies, distractions, and disorders.

Higher insight and love

An important aspect of changing the underlying dynamics of personality is a better understanding of love. Through observation, I have found that love, in many forms, can be described as a fluid state that seeks stability, but does not find it. Never the less, this lack of support does not seem to damage or disturb the state of love. Instead, a secondary state finds the instability pleasurable, creating a sensation of almost floating.

Depending on the personality and qualities of the experiencer, there will be positive, complex, difficult, or other types of perceptions that cascade from this state causing other perceptions to arise. The results might even include previously established learned behaviors, such as controlling, jealousy, or even false self-abnegation to gain the favor of their object of love.

As the mind continues its energetic attempt to bond to an object, not only does it seek to know this object, but desires or craves to be the subject of that love object. However, to sustain love feelings, this continual pleasurable attempt should, oddly enough, never find satisfaction and must remain in an unfulfilled dynamic. Once love-curiosity-grasping is satisfied, either there will be a drop in love followed by a falling out of love feeling, or the relationship dynamics will change.

Feelings of closeness, companionship, careful familiarity, and respect are encouraged in psychology to help relationships mature and survive when the curiosity phase ends in an intimate relationship. An immature lover always wishes to be perceived as the admired object of love. As a more mature lover changes and experiences a drop in pleasure/curiosity feelings, they will automatically desire a new kind of connection. If this important shift happens for one partner before the other, this could be a factor in separation and divorce.

Loving hobbies such as Buddhism

Another form of love dynamic might be experienced, for example, in love of photography, a collection of brass spittoons, or even "love" of duck hunting. However, hobbies and objects are usually quite easily known by completing a course of study, going duck hunting a number of times or acquiring a number of brass spittoons and researching their details diligently. After a short time, the mystery is gone.

When the object is known to a certain satisfaction, that form of obsessive grasping "love" will disappear or substantially subside. Hobbies or interests that we might feel are all consuming and stimulate a gripping desire to know more can suddenly become stale and uninteresting. Perhaps the possibilities of enjoying and feeling that kind of love will again rise as you discover a new hobby. Perhaps your obsessive love will fix next upon inkwells and their every detail, or perhaps even Buddhism.

However, if we approach Buddhism as a hobby, then it will have the qualities of a hobby, stimulating interest to satisfy our emotional curiosity. In spite of the lower quality wish to enter the study of Buddhism as a new hobby, the very nature of the Great Path of Dharma teachings is complex, dear, and impossible to know definitively. These are all characteristics necessary for a long-term love relationship. In addition, the systematic trainings in the teachings and Buddha nature by one's root mentor or bodhisattva inner mentor are alive in great love toward us. Because of this, a new form of love arises in practitioners by this blessed design. The deep, never-ending qualities of practice, related concepts such as loving kindness, and virtuous objects should stimulate our minds for our whole lifetime and beyond. In that way, love for practice only grows and never declines.

Love in the personal liberation vehicle

In the Hinayana practice of personal liberation the correct relationship with one's own mind requires watchfulness and readiness to discipline. In that tradition, withdrawal from sensory experience is strongly emphasized so that there is less data to process. The fluid, mind-bending states of love inherent in the Mahayana altruistic wish to save all sentient beings are not so compatible with the discipline needed for Hinayana practice.

An anonymous Hinayana monk warns us of the negativities inherent in love: "*If, through our own ripening knowledge, we appreciate that our ultimate and highest purpose should be Nirvana, the absolute end of sorrow, then all goals beneath that are cast in a new light. When we have something to live for that is higher than fame, honor, friendship, or health, higher even than love, we can never be utterly impoverished or ruined. We are in fact in a much better position to enjoy what ever may be achieved in worldly life because we no longer depend solely on changeable circumstances for our happiness.*"

This monk is looking at love in a way that differs from how we have explored it so far. His position is the same as that of the Mahayana, or greater vehicle, in the first of its three paths of training. His perspective is correct from the outlook of the first Yana, or first path, the Hinayana. The Mahayana contains the Hinayana trainings as preliminaries, and the Vajrayana, or path of transformative energetic practices, contains all three in a specific order without disrespecting any stage.

Love in the Mahayana altruistic vehicle

The emphasis in Western psychology is to bring the unhappy person to a state of self-acceptance and self-love so they are able to tolerate the stresses of everyday life without behaving badly. Gaining self-confidence, this naturally leads to new levels of happiness in self-discovery and one begins to include others in that state of self-love. This leads to eventual great errors at the time of analysis of reality to transcend to a new way of being. This error is compounded by believing that there is a beneficial state where, (now unconsciously), the believer gathers others in an ever extending network of me.

In contrast, from the beginning, the Mahayana path of altruistic responsibility presents us another love object by first training the new Buddhist practitioner in loving-kindness, development of altruistic love toward others and forgetting their "own needs". Mahayanists grow by learning to love others as their own precious mother from a previous life in order to establish others as dear. Removing self-cherishing in this way not only produces a high state of well-being, happiness, and self-confidence, but is directly connected to higher process in evolution toward enlightenment.

The Buddha counseled his son: *"Rahula, practice loving-kindness to overcome anger."* In Buddhist scriptures, throughout the actual training facilitated by the outer mentor and in your own studies and meditation, loving-kindness is extremely important. The Buddha training his own son: *"Loving-kindness has the capacity to bring happiness to others without demanding anything in return."*

By training in this way, we establish expanded parameters on our love, overwhelming the bad habit of seeking love in order to possess another, by weaning us away from wrong perceptions of love as a personal possession. We also become capable of breaking inappropriate bonds between the perception of love and the concepts of anger, jealousy, or even violence. The consequences of perceptual crossed wires are dreadful. For example, video game players might learn to connect violence and sex or violence and love. Crossed wires such as this are present and sometimes even encouraged by rough, modern society. Bonding the dynamics of sex and love can prevent higher forms of love from arising, and forms that are more animalistic in nature become the norm. Poor strategies, such as wanting to possess another, also create confusion in others and ourselves. We may even try to make our partner obey us so we can give them our love.

Love of study and practice

Another way that love is present in higher Buddhist practices is love of study. A love-excitement keeps us interested in pursuing difficult subjects, such as emptiness, or commentaries of famous Buddhist scholars of the past. We enjoy applying the teachings to our personal practice without tiring because there is so much to learn. We feel drawn to drink from the well of understanding until we are filled, then meditate and review our understanding, and return to drink deeply again. During the entire process, whether actively studying or processing and integrating what we have learned, we never lose our thirst, feel satisfied, or feel a need to take a rest from study to refresh ordinary mind. The very thing that we do not want to do, is reactivate ordinary concepts.

Someone told me a story about a monk who was in strict three-year retreat, except every six weeks for three hours, he would leave his retreat to have tea with a friend and take a break from retreat. He said he found it quite helpful to have worldly interaction with his friend for three hours before going back into his retreat place for another six weeks.

In contrast, during study time, we always remained connected to our studies because, as much as possible, we did not want to contaminate our education with ordinary concepts. We remained "in love" with study and did not want to break the connection between ourselves and the well of learning and wisdom. In addition, when we activate love feelings toward study, enlightened beings will encourage us with blessings and inner guidance.

Love of our Buddhist practice changes our view of what is important and what is not. We might even experience special secret delight in seeing our meditation cushion, our altar objects, or even our mala prayer beads. We treat this delight respectfully, without false sophistication. We avoid the cynicism that might creep in by thinking '*Oh, how silly of me, I am acting like a kid.*' Let us maintain a nice love relationship with our Buddhist meditation practice. Maybe sometimes you could even hug your mala. Personally, it delights me inside to express joy of practice in fresh and innocent ways.

Our thankas and prayer beads

A meditator who is uncertain about what is sacred might experience anxiety about their practice objects, such as who do I allow to touch them, are they good enough quality, or otherwise imbue them with solidification. In order to overcome these and other issues regarding our own Buddhist objects, we are trained to understand that even things we love as part of our practice only arise in dependence upon causes and conditions, and are empty of self nature by being naturally without essence.

However, because of our love for our practice, we do not reject them as being without value, with confusion regarding their emptiness and instead might affirm, *"This is my mala, the mala of my practice, and you want to take away my mala? I will keep my mala. Why? I need my mala because it is useful, and it is part of my practice."* You might look around, *'Oh, if someone walked in the door right now and saw me hugging my meditation cushion, what would they think?'"*

The point here is to create an attitude that is delicate and balanced. We do not cling toward the objects of practice such as thankas and images, but we do need to have a kind of love that acts as a support for delight in our practice objects. On the other hand, we do not need to collect many dharma objects to demonstrate our love of our practice and objects of practice.

We make strong efforts to avoid contaminating our intimate love relationship with practice by feeling that we have learned enough or reached an advanced level where we have gotten all that is possible to get out of the practice. That means we never give up our Buddhist refuge vows in the three jewels, Buddha, the dharma path to enlightenment and sangha, the enlightened community. We also never give up bodhichitta, the wish to be of benefit to all sentient beings.

With skillful behaviors and pure love toward our cultivated Buddhist values and careful perceptions, when the time arises for you to automatically enter a lower Nirvana of cessation, will you say, *"I will give up my bodhichitta if that is what is the best thing for me to do."* No, we will need to have values so ingrained that they become personal strengths. We must not be "on again-off again" regarding values affirmed as a support for awakening by others who have already entered the enlightened state. To be dependable and trustworthy in maintaining values that will produce the energetic support for our inner process to the enlightened state is called samaya.

The dog's tooth

An interesting story comes from the Lam Rim (Tibetan for Stages of the Path) by Je Pabonka Rinpoche... In Tibet, a very simple peasant woman had a son departing for India on a trading trip. As he is leaving, she requests him with folded hands, *"Now you are going to India, you might not go ever again, and I am old already. You please bring me back a tooth relic of the Buddha so that I can place it on my altar and make offerings. That is all that I want."*

As the son is returning from India, he realizes that he has completely forgotten his mother's request. He also knows that it is patently absurd to be able to find a tooth of Lord Buddha Shakyamuni as these relics are rare and the few remaining are encased in stupa reliquaries in holy places.

He is almost home when he sees the rotting remains of a dead dog at the side of the road. Reaching down he easily pulls out a tooth from the head of the dead dog, wipes it off, wraps it in a clean napkin, and continues home where his mother is waiting to greet him. *"Hello my son. Did you bring me the tooth relic of the Buddha?"*

"Of course I did dear mother and here it is." With great delight, she immediately placed it on the altar and began to make extensive offerings, many prayers, and many rejoicings.

The son was reticent to tell her that this was a dog's tooth and as time went on, he began to feel increasingly guilty that he had done this and fooled his mother so badly. He was at the point of telling her about his lie, *"You know that tooth that I brought you..."* She, with great delight, showed him the tooth on the altar, glowing with inner light. It was the Buddha's tooth after all.

Upon the basis of a dog's tooth and faith, she soon attained enlightenment. What to say about consecrated practices offered to you from an unbroken lineage directly from Lord Buddha? Beyond that, what we bring to our practice in faith, motivation, love, and dedication is what we get out of the practice by attainment of valuable personal standards. However, if we instead feel that we have gotten everything that we could out of the practice, and the practice is vast, deep, powerful, transformative, and blessed, then certainly it is not a lack coming from the side of the practice.

Vast wishes for all sentient beings

Sharing happiness with all living beings such as in the Four Great Wishes trains us in giving love and joy without holding it as a personal possession. The second of the Four Great Wishes, wanting to end suffering for all living beings, instills in us a deep love of order and alignment due to wishing for others to enter more evolved ways of being. The buddhas and bodhisattvas support our vast wishes based on superior principles.

This is an even more pure altruistic love based upon understanding the illusory manner in which things exist. Suffering, by nature, is a misalignment with the way living beings actually exist. We learn to become tireless in our efforts to end suffering by arising bodhichitta compassion but we will not end suffering by suffering ourselves. Instead, because it feels so good, so pleasurable to experience the desire to end suffering, our wanting to end suffering is no suffering at all for us!

The third of the four great wishes is that all sentient beings experience bliss without the stain of the confusion of the innate view that takes the transitory to be permanent. This immense wish connects us to a love and value of perfection; certainly a suitable object for an evolving sense of refuge and love.

However, we should not allow our intellectual understanding of the magnificence of perfection to degenerate into ordinary worldly demands for perfection, something that this world is not capable of giving. In addition, wishing all sentient beings to experience bliss also destroys the contaminated basis for our own suffering.

Equanimity, the fourth of the four great wishes, destroys racism and specism, so we do not damage or discourage this ability to love others by becoming dry and scholarly in our approach to life and spiritual practice. Encouragement from advanced meditators and those who have entered the enlightened state is alive, juicy, and expectant with healthy love energies that inspire, guide, and direct us toward transformation and perfection.

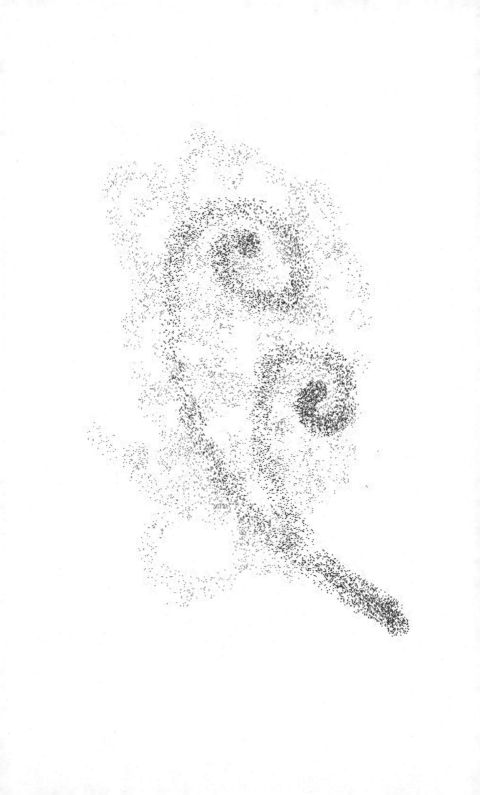

Chapter 16
Emptiness and Protecting Our Love

"The high Dharma of the Victorious Ones
Is a goldmine of happiness for all beings;
And you, my son, are its fearless keeper—
I pray you may reign for a thousand years.
When the note touched my hand
The wind of your immaculate deeds
Swept up the cotton wisp of my mind
And carried my thoughts to you there"

Je Tsongktapa's Epistle to Ngawang Drakpa

Experience in mind training such as putting into practice the aphorisms of the seven points by Geshe Chekawa makes us more capable and qualified to enter into the study of the nature of reality. Then the powerful teachings on lack of inherent existence and the wonderful simplicity of the explanation of emptiness can cause a sudden shift inside that is a sign of meaningful change. Preparation and cogitation accomplished on the deep inquiry and analysis of the twenty emptinesses of Chandrakirti gives us permission to enter into cultivated inner dynamics described in the treatise and commentary. Long-time, skillful meditators will deliberately enter into the state without foundation three or four times a day in order to make the mind flelxible for the actual transformative event.

In their quest for perfection in their own being by creating benefit for others, helper beings, such as learner bodhisattvas, rest their minds in a place away from the chaos of conflicted energies of the sense bases of the meditator. Since the meditator is in active transition, there are cleansings and purifications of energetic clutter and dust accumulated that the inner bodhisattva does not need to experience.

However, as soon as the meditator is capable, he or she is expected to be meditating in the higher-level practices, accomplishing self purifications, and moving into a place without foundation without becoming overly fascinated. These systematic processes will eventually recreate the meditator into someone capable of receiving high teachings on the actual interior without the confusion of the ordinary senses.

Integrate knowledge- relax body and mind on the path

In that way, I hope this commentary on Chandrakirti's Twenty Emptiness will become a valuable resource for you to review and put into practice. Even if you should be in conversation with someone who has been Buddhist for 20 or 30 years, please do not feel that you do not have the correct information or that something was missing in this explanation. I qualify that by stating that there are many important commentaries regarding emptiness that have become classics in Buddhism. This means that I have not hidden anything out of a sense of secret pride. However, there remains much that space here does not permit to be fully explained and future books will focus on other reasoning and concepts regarding this important subject.

Many believe that the study of emptiness is far more complicated than it actually is. I hope the explanations given in this book will help you understand, and be able to discuss these concepts intelligently with anyone. You will also be capable of understanding and applying strong mental force against the disfigurements of this world and feel victorious.

Those who are adept in this process always feel that this world is not so complicated as others complain that it is, and they do not enter into the suffering dynamics that ordinary people do. Whether you are sick or well, whether good luck is coming or bad luck is coming, whether you are getting what you want or you are not getting what you want; there should be no reason that your mind should ever be disturbed again. This is a sign of putting mind training into practice. This ease and joy is also a sign of holding the view that understands that a state without foundation is the aligned resting place of the mind. One reason it is called emptiness is that it is devoid of characteristics causing ordinary human mind and human consciousness to suffer. It is a dispersal of ordinary mind.

The membrane separates ordinary mind

However, for those entering who are familiar with this resting place, it is simply an antechamber to a more aligned way of being. A washing away of all perceptions changes the membrane that holds ordinary beings away from interaction with enlightened society while they are infected with the insanity of ordinary mind.

However, before transformation, the membrane between outer and inner minds could become damaged. Some damage it with drugs, others use machines built to bypass this membrane with automatic meditation devices and some people misuse their minds with inappropriate meditations. In all these and more cases, the person taking an easy path, literally could be accessing what they should not know, do not have permission to know and are not yet prepared to know.

The systematic reproducible path of preparation for transformation gives us tools such as compassion and logic to integrate into practice so that it produces the powerful transformative effect. One important point that should be remembered is, do not disturb your own mind, and do not distract your delicate inner process from preparation for transformation. Over a very long time, perhaps you have become so accustomed to annoying yourself it feels normal, and that needs to change.

A natural decay of the membranes is accomplished with developing levels of trust from inner minds that are beginning to feel more comfortable. As the push and pull of aversion and attraction is reduced in the outer mind, we can relax a bit to stabilize new perceptions and begin to enjoy the human realm in a new way that is both refreshing and healing.

Life is like scents wafting on the breeze. Out in the countryside, you can smell the cows, and then a moment later the breeze shifts and you can no longer smell the cows and now it smells like hay. Soon your attention notices that from over there comes the smell of fresh bread. In that way, your awareness attention is drawn to a continuous circulation of different kinds of energetic stimuli. If we tried to prevent smelling the cow by doing something to the cow or retard the hay's ability to produce an odor, we would be acting like ordinary people who only want to experience nice smells or happiness. Instead, we need to become accustomed to feeling satisfied with whatever is happening and stop struggling to only wish to gather happiness.

Strengthen by personal responsibility

For seekers of happiness, the demands that ordinary people place on God and higher beings to fix everything bothering them are not an effective use of spiritual connections. The general duty of the inner wisdom bodhisattva is facilitating in many different ways the return to alignment with perfection.

We need to mature and take responsibility by reducing the delusions and grasping after ephemeral happiness. We are presented with new opportunities, through our relationship to the bodhisattvas, to enter into higher training toward perfection. This valuable connection to enlightened being interior exposes us to wisdom and emptiness in a way that is valid, safe, and guided.

In order to be capable of receiving training, we need to strengthen our spiritual muscles, discrimination, and understand the larger process toward transformation without wasting time by entertaining evanescent mental wanderings of fantasy. Stabilizing in knowledge of how things actually exist should cause us to feel empowered to deal with difficulties that act as real obstacles to development. We should not waste our lives in trying to fix what is so ephemeral such as the stench of cows and hay wafting across the fields. As we take interest in personal responsibility and take care of what is important, we can come alive in higher development.

Power of love

Understanding and meditating on the   dynamic which combines love with appreciation of our precious human life makes us capable of the unusual attitude of deriving pleasure from not knowing. Then a love dynamic that we feel toward study, our Buddhist practice, and even love toward our prayer beads helps our progress, and we always feel happy.

An ability to fall in love with meditation, the Buddha, and practice is given to us in lieu of the correct inner sense of fully developed compassion-love of the mature bodhisattva. This is a correct transitional stage of development because our potential for love is tremendous.

In young people, the discovery of their potential for love and care in the form of an actual physical closeness almost takes away their ability to see. A strong inward gaze of physiological self interest or obsession, as well as nervous system arousal, combined with a feeling that every part of the body is alive with this gripping wanting to know, is directed toward the efforts to possess the object of love.

A powerful, driving force of obsession and curiosity looking at itself is also the tremendous energy source of creativity, art, and poetry. Many important essentials of human life are established by an ability to love in its many forms, binding others to yourself as part of your human identity. There is also a potential of damaging your ability to love. Some will substitute damaged emotions for a clear human potential for love.

Denying themselves the preparations for a more mature and then even higher love, some instead develop misguided trust and distrust. If these are not healed, it turns into fear, and through that, an unknown cascade of negative emotions can arise, damaging further the precious human life possibilities for preparation for enlightenment. Disappointments in love should not be allowed to damage our natural ability to love, and yet that is how we feel. Often, the usual reaction is to decide that now we should be very careful with everyone because we have been disappointed. The object of our love has rejected us, and now we feel pain and disappointment even while continuing to experience the after effects of love once our love object has departed.

This needs to be healed by authentic practice with more valid love objects. We can rely on the Buddha, the teachings toward perfection, and the great body of enlightened companions who have already been through what you have been through, or even worse, but are now healed and ready to assist you as bodhisattvas!

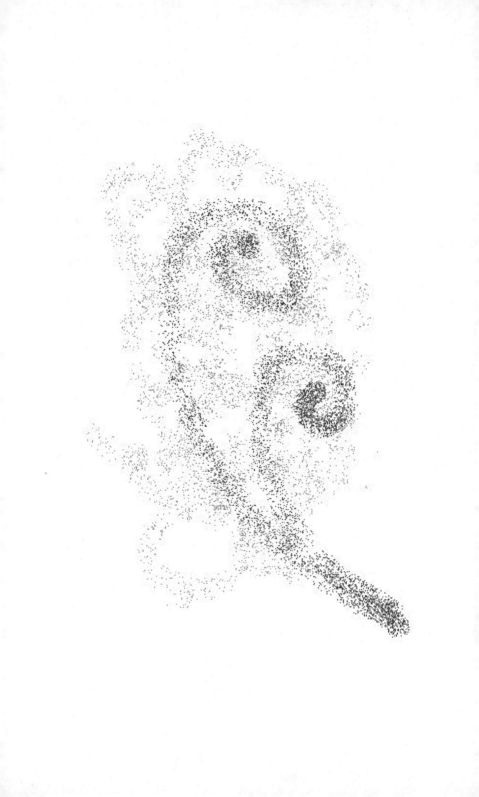

Chapter 17
Emptiness and Altruistic Love

*"The sun's great rays shine everywhere, traveling like
a horse-drawn chariot. The ground supports the world
without calculating the burden. Such is the nature of
persons of great capacity, who lack any self interest; They
are consumed with whatever brings happiness and benefit
to the world."*

Chandragomin's Letter to a Student

We want to know and experience true love, and we derive
pleasure when, unable to possess it, we still maintain a
constant flow toward the object. Depending on the nature and
development of the person, the object could be an individual,
a hobby, or Buddhist study. In the higher practices, we
learn to maintain an intimate relationship with the objects
of our Buddhist studies, such as bodhichitta, emptiness, or
other cultivated attitudes needed for transformation and
destruction of obstacles.

Love contains a capacity to maintain a kind of *"not
knowing"* that helps us hold steady in our desire to maintain
the emotion by not owning the object of love while still
maintaining contact. Without the ability to endure through
our natural tendency to change our mind regularly, we
would be in love and then a moment later fall out of love,
then again in love, then fall away once more.

Even in ordinary, mature interpersonal relationships, there must be continuity, a steady undercurrent, developed and cultivated, coming from a deeper place than the changeable mental functions. Therefore, even though we have received the bestowal of love continuity within the complex programming of a human innate view, combined with a commitment to hold through difficult times, it is still our obligation to cultivate the ability to love steadily. Through this practice, we will continue to expand and develop our capacity to get along with many others while increasing our understanding of how to do so skillfully. Eventually, we will realize altruistic loving kindness and the great capacity for getting along with all others.

Loving kindness
and the state without foundation

In higher trainings, the steady flow of inner guidance toward awakening, connected to a growing desire for higher-level objects, such as buddhas and bodhisattva inner mentor, is the result of training in loving-kindness. These emerging higher ethical values motivate us to become proficient through study and practice that, in turn, make us steady in our efforts to be of benefit to myriad living beings in the exquisite manner of our own inner mentor.

Mental steadiness produces a calm and happy state that prevents us from disturbing our own mind so that we can experience a new form of love energy bestowal coming from our own mind, inner minds, and inner mentor. This further increases our capacity to love, which is again applied toward study and practice. This pleasurable and beneficial cycle continues for a very long time.

The next steps of maintaining a steady mind and motivation are supported by many restful interludes in the state without foundation. Renewing the mind in this way allows us to return refreshed each time to human activity and understanding and makes better use of the human bestowal of increased capacity for love while on the Path to the enlightened state. We then become more balanced in the intellectual mind, knowing more deeply by familiarity that a state without foundation does exist. Through the many glimpses into that state and the encouragement from outer mentor, study and meditation, as well as becoming even more attracted to the foundationless state, deeper support for practice is realized.

Such is the inner process of a person in training for a career as a bodhisattva. Their development is based in altruistic love for all living beings. Of course, for the best results, altruistic love for all sentient beings must be instilled in the practitioner by stages from the beginning by first taking vows of bodhchitta and promising to attain enlightenment not for one's own sake, but for the sake of all others.

Natural altruism

It is possible that you could already have a natural ability to love altruistically. Perhaps you arrived in this world with a cultivated understanding of love from transformational process in some previous life during which the training was begun, but not completed. If that ability remains undamaged by worldly contact, as soon as you come into connect with the teachings, you will easily remember your previous training and be able to express altruistic love toward the correct object, all sentient beings. However, even beings with a more advanced inner nature from previous lives will also need to experientially review the step-by-step process of understanding the actual nature of altruistic love, beginning with loving-kindness.

Those who do not arrive in this world with developed altruistic motivation can still practice loving-kindness. This social lubricant of the world does not hurt you in any way; it helps you, and it helps others. It is easy to understand this because, when others show loving-kindness toward you, it is very easy to act with loving-kindness toward them in return. However, if you have loving-kindness toward them, and they respond by giving you a hard time, you still have an opportunity to practice genuine loving-kindness, patience, and compassion toward them.

At this point in development, it is typical to be presented with new ways of looking at situations that are contrary to the worldly view and powerfully beneficial, such as love and compassion returned for difficulty. We learn that altruistic love does not depend upon receiving good feedback in order to feel appreciated. If we crave appreciation, it is no longer altruistic love, but ordinary love, a kind of buying and selling of favors. Steady love results from training in emptiness and understanding the suffering, illusory nature of ordinary reality. With this deep understanding, we will wish to free others as if they were trapped in a burning building.

Overcoming obstacles to altruistic love

We should not allow contamination of our ability to understand or increase altruistic love by becoming disappointed when others do not appreciate our altruism or think that it is no use to practice it. In order to avoid that obstacle, we begin with loving-kindness rather than trying to feel ultimate compassion. We remember that if we feel disappointed or angry with people while, for example, performing dharma service, we can always go to the fallback position of gentle loving-kindness. However, we should never give less than loving-kindness.

We also need to temper grasping while love still remains strong. We can practice in harmony with the Hinayana ideals of abandoning grasping where the practitioner is destined to enter cessation, where both love and grasping disappear together. However, in the Mahayana, we must sustain a new balance of decreased grasping while love is still active. We place love high in our practice and continue to increase our desire to save all living beings, and this makes us juicy and dear to others, who are attracted toward us.

Holding all sentient beings in the heart

The attractive quality coming from inside us creates new and stronger connections to others so that, in the future, they will benefit as we become more capable. As we experience less grasping while Mahayana love still remains, we receive powerful bestowals from the buddhas and bodhisattvas that strengthen our abilities and help us stabilize positive, healthy attitudes. The safest method of stabilizing is the practice of holding all sentient beings in your heart of hearts as dear.

When beings are no longer "*out there*" because they are "*here*" in your heart, a new intimate relationship arises based on equanimity toward all living beings without regard for individual characteristics. Likewise, it will not matter whether they have benefited us or not. Now, love is not mixed with contaminated outer universal energies or the confused mental energies of others. Though we remain in human form, identity has moved more interior and is protected from many potential harms

Repairing contaminated energies

As you probably already know, this world is not a pureland; therefore, there are unaligned energies moving in our world in abundance. Our attempts to align what is discordant to a healthy new way of being are like trying to fix a wound when the blood has already spilled and is exposed and contaminated. Perhaps we could try to collect the spilt blood in a bottle, mix it with some bleach to remove all the red color and push it back inside the body. This would be like trying to align contaminated universal outer energies once they have escaped into this denser place. It is no use.

Once blood has left the closed system of a body, it is not the clean substance that it was inside the body. It has now escaped and mixed with dust, air, and molecules from other substances. We may have to put it in a centrifuge and extrapolate its little corpuscles in order to make it clean enough to put back inside. We might have to boil the blood too. I am just joking, but this is a serious subject. Once life force inner energies escape *"out there,"* they become changed, so we need new strategies to purify ourselves.

Sentient beings are near and dear to us

Chandrakirti says that reality is not the way we perceive it. Therefore, we should avoid stimulating mental confusion, and instead train steadily in the view that all sentient beings are as near and dear as our own mothers. When we train in this method, in conjunction with study and meditation on emptiness, compassion, and other important elements of preparation for awakening, we bond healthy concepts together for an increasingly comprehensive view.

We acknowledge deeply that living beings in their entirety are dear, believing that, 'my heart of hearts is the safest place for them to reside.' That is valuable because, if we hold them dear, we will never hurt them. We do not want to depend on the unreliable and unstable influence of the innate view because it is not the excellent filter for our interactions with the world, nor for the world's interactions with us.

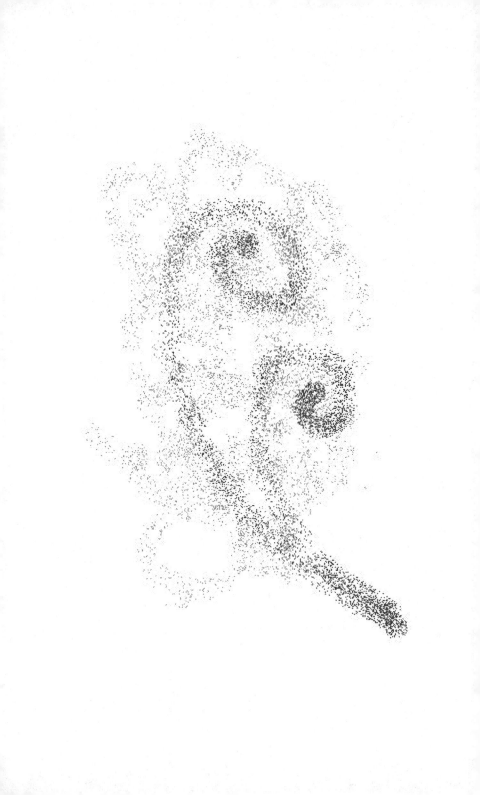

Chapter 18
Emptiness and Bliss: Mystery Solved

"In the space of bliss-void inseparable
Amidst wondrous clouds of infinite offerings
Is the tree that grants our every wish,
Adorned with flowers, leaves, and fruit.
At its crown, on a lion throne ablaze with jewels,
You sit on a lotus, sun, and full moon, my Root Guru,
Kind in three ways, the essence of all Buddhas"
Lama Chopa Offering to the Spiritual Guide

Perfection is possible and is unrestricted, able to arise in any form in any realm to guide others. Perfection, in the hidden guise of an authentic teacher showing us the way to enlightenment, is also capable of appearing in inner and outer forms, reminding us, giving teachings and calling us to our true home when we become lost.

The actual student and recipient of care is deep interior to the outer person and is more energetic in nature than conscious human thinking. However, it understands energetics far more complex than the human mind can process. If the preparation for a quantum shift in consciousness is done correctly, the inner being experiences a correct love dynamic that it cannot understand, but is attracted to, in its own far more sophisticated method. When this happens, a powerfully pleasurable, even blissful, effect in its own subtle inner being arises.

We experience this activity as bliss in the outer mind because something is happening in the inner minds that we cannot process in our usual methods. The normal ways of discerning meaning gleaned from information fail in this case. Even the close inner minds, such as the subconscious, are not able to process bliss as correct understanding of wisdom, but instead experience extreme pleasure.

The innermost subtle mind, where the actual essence being resides in the place of its deepest development, may or may not be able to understand bliss as teachings relating to the next method in which it will be alive. The innermost essence actual being, however, is not a passive recipient of these dense and comprehensive teachings, but is open, wishing to absorb as much as possible of the marvelous teachings of perfection's activities and care. The actual inner being, the receptive aspect of the real you inside, was created to crave to know perfection, and is the one that experiences the blissful true love teachings in the form of inner union.

Healing by bliss

As the actual being becomes stimulated, a cascade of healing effects occurs in its being like a shiver. Through the process of manifestation by emanation, an opening begins from the interior actual being, spreading through various levels of inner mind that also experience this effect in their own way. Through this process, inner minds can experience what the actual being is now producing. In fact, they cannot prevent experiencing change as the byproduct of this innermost union with bliss. If all goes well, a surge of inner teachings heading toward your outer mind will pass easily through various membranes presently held in a careful configuration for later development.

Yogis describe themselves as "we yogis, seekers of bliss," not out of a sense of wishing to experience sensual pleasure, but because they seek the nature of reality, altruistic love and joy. Each of these elements are preliminary to arisal of special bliss that will prepare the yogi to experience even higher bliss stages. In other words, when we no longer hold the grasping, contaminated view, we become capable of experiencing the supreme events possible for a human being.

The early stages of bliss and emptiness are still held back from the experience of enlightenment itself by their contaminated view. The glimpses and introductions to bliss will become even stronger yet, and this marks a powerful entry into the practices where inner teachings will be received. When we enter, we will no longer have the confusion of unaligned perceptions to grasp onto and will no longer be prevented from continuously experiencing the state of bliss-love, the flow of teachings.

The bliss dynamic is an advanced and vital part of development. A sign of entering a certain level of an enlightened state is passing days and nights in bliss without wishing to rise from it. A continuous flow of inner teachings completely envelops and captivates the mind at this stage of development. A full immersion in bliss is often what occurs in samadhi trance states, when even the outer breath is drawn inward with the awareness. However, once the innate view is destroyed and the capacity to understand the bliss teachings arises, we will no longer experience bliss so strongly because another kind of knowing stage has been achieved.

Bonding Bliss and Emptiness

Love and emptiness, a true compassion state, and bliss and emptiness, the drawing together and training of yogic energies, are both correct states of mind gathered in the ancient methods of deliberate transformation by interior guidance. Now that we have bonded these concepts together, we need to maintain this connection.

While experiencing bliss energies, we must sustain the connection with a receptive aspect of love from our side; otherwise, we would literally be trying to rape bliss in order to get it. This attack on bliss indicates a still immature and aggressive wish to control; it is self-cherishing and wrong.

The correct love dynamic that allows the mind to remain in a pleasurable and active state of receptivity will also be actively receiving embedment of new perceptions, causing us to be capable of knowing bliss correctly. We become an actual holder of the deep inner teachings. Bliss-love, the alert-receptive dynamic that finds pleasure in not possessing the object, now in its maturity, allows us to maintain a connection with higher development while ordinary mind is held correctly in the state without foundation during samadhi trances.

Dynamic redux of bliss-love

A penetration of inner mind with deeper awareness energies often produces sexual imagery in the conscious mind that adds energy and redirects the root center energies into the inner opening. These root center energies are liquefied and drawn into a dynamic redux activated by inner mentor, something that neither the inner being nor outer being can do. Redux means restored to consciousness, life, or vigor. This change does not require sex or sexual imagery, although sexual imagery has been used in this process for a very long time.

In conclusion, the entry of bliss-love into the dynamic of emptiness should happen smoothly and without disfiguring either concept. We do not release energetic understanding of emptiness in order to be able to experience bliss-love.

In addition, it is correct to understand that bliss-love does not require emptiness in order to exist; likewise, emptiness can be experienced without bliss-love. However, it is not a good idea to separate these higher-level concepts because our experience of emptiness is now being trained to bond to the altruistic.

This is where the two correct states of compassion and energetic yogic training converge. When this bond is created correctly, we will emerge from a special induced state not as candidates for cessation, but as candidates for higher trainings toward Buddhahood. However, if this is done unskillfully, we will enter cessation, the lower liberation. This would be a great loss. Our human realm needs many more benefit beings in order to sustain this world for future beings who will require a safe and pure place to practice and prepare for their transformation and higher trainings.

You are already experienced in the human realm and its challenges, and you thoroughly understand the problems that you have faced on your journey up to this point in development toward awakening. Altruistic great love and the understanding of reality will recreate you as a benefit being for the human realm. Then, in the future, when you are offered cessation, you will state with confidence, "*I do not accept. I have work to do for the benefit of all sentient beings*" and that, dear friends, is the answer to the mystery of emptiness and love.